FACHAUSDRÜCKE IM KUNSTGEWERBE	GLOSARIO DE TÉRMINOS DE ARTESANÍA
Korbflechterei	Cestería
Buchbinderei	Encuadernación
Goldschnitt, Goldpressung	dorado
Kaligraphie	caligrafía
Keramik	Cerámica
Töpferware	alfarería
Steinware, Steingut	barró
Töpferware, irdenes Geschirr	loza
Porzellan	porcelana
Skulptur	escultura
emaillieren	esmaltar
Kacheln	azulejo
auf der Töpferscheibe geformt	hecho en torno
Konstruktion	construcción
Platte	losa
Glas	Vidrio
Glas blasen	soplar vidrio
geformtes Glas	vidrio amoldado
Buntglas	vidriera
Mosaik	mosaico
Lederarbeit	Cuero
bossieren	repujado
Lederstickerei	cuero bordado
Bereitung (für Buchbinderei)	preparación del cuero
Überzug (Schachteln)	guarnición
Metallarbeit	Latería
Gold und Silber Schmiedearbeit	platería
Messingarbeit	latón
Schmiedeeisen	hierro forjado
Schmuck	joyería
emaillieren	esmaltar
Zellenschmelz	cloisonné

(Fortsetzung auf dem hinteren Einbandblatt) *(Sigue en la última página)*

THE CRAFTS OF THE MODERN WORLD

THE CRAFTS OF THE MODERN WORLD

EDITED BY ROSE SLIVKA

with 405 illustrations and texts by

AILEEN O. WEBB

ROSE SLIVKA

MARGARET MERWIN PATCH

published by

HORIZON PRESS **NEW YORK** *in collaboration with the* **WORLD CRAFTS COUNCIL**

ACKNOWLEDGMENTS

To all those craftsmen and craft organizations, both government and private, whose worldwide contributions of photographs and data have helped create the archives of the World Crafts Council and made publication of this book possible.

To UNESCO for its constant encouragement and assistance to the World Crafts Council and for permission to use data from the report "World Crafts—A Mid-20th Century Survey" which was prepared for UNESCO by the World Crafts Council.

To CRAFT HORIZONS magazine, The Museum of Contemporary Crafts and the Research and Education Department of the American Craftsmen's Council, which contributed so generously of their photographic files.

To Jan McDevitt, Mary Lyon, Kit Bradshaw, Ann Berryman, and Patricia Dandignac for painstaking editorial assistance, meticulous attention to infinite technical detail, and insight into the specialized problems of researching and selecting the material.

To Aileen O. Webb, president of the World Crafts Council, whose unswerving commitment to the world of crafts and conviction in the need for this book gave impetus to its publication and made possible its international scope.

R.S.

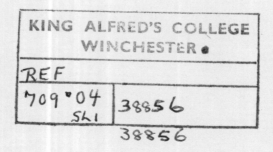

CONTENTS

INDEX TO ILLUSTRATIONS (Grouped by Continent)

6

CRAFTS IN THE MODERN WORLD : A Preface

by Aileen O. Webb

The wisdom of a scribe cometh by opportunity of leisure: and he that hath little business shall become wise.

So every carpenter and master builder that laboreth night and day: and they that cut and grave seals and are diligent to make great variety, who give themselves to make a life-like picture, and whose sleepless care is to finish a work.

So the smith, sitting by the anvil and tiring himself with the rough iron: the smoke of the fire wasteth his flesh, and he fighteth with the heat of the furnace: The noise of the anvil deafens his ears, and his eyes are upon the pattern of the utensil: he giveth his mind to finish his work, and his sleepless care is to polish it perfectly.

So the potter sitting at his work, and turning the wheel about with his feet, who is always anxious about his work, and maketh his work by number. He fashioneth the clay with his arm, and maketh it pliable with his feet; he applieth himself to glaze it over: and his sleepless care is to make clean the furnace.

All these trust to their hands, and every one is wise in his work.

Without these shall not a city be inhabited: And men shall not dwell abroad, nor go up and down:

They shall not be sought for in public council, nor sit high in the congregation: they shall not sit in the judge's seat, nor understand the statutes of the covenant: they shall not declare justice and they shall not be found where parables are spoken.

But they will maintain the world,
And their prayer be for the work of their craft.

—The Wisdom of Jesus, Ecclesiasticus

In the wake of the vast technological revolution, which began towards the close of the nineteenth century, the world has largely forgotten that there are still millions of human beings who live by the use of their hands alone. There is no area in which craftsmen are not found—from the igloos of the Eskimos to unknown African villages, from the hillsides of Japan to the Andean mountains of South America, from the busy towns of Europe and North America to a quiet hamlet in Nepal—craftsmanship weaves an intricate and fascinating net of creative endeavor. The prevailing spirit of the men who have always done this work is expressed by the Apocryphal passage that heads this page. The significant line is: "But they will maintain the world."

It is the creative spirit of man, expressed in a thousand different ways, that pushes him forward and this it is that makes craftsmanship so important in the present industrial sweep of our society. The history of mankind is epitomized by this work on view in all the museums of the world.

This volume is, we believe, the first of its kind ever published on contemporary crafts the world over. It demonstrates that the varying environments of men are reflected in their work. A study of the photographs gives a panorama of the backgrounds against which the work was made.

Inevitably, the interacting influences of time, place and individual temperament have developed a great variety of craft activities. One finds artist-craftsmen who do only individual one-of-a-kind pieces, who exhibit and have a great influence on changing styles. Designer-craftsmen also produce individual work of great quality but will often produce a piece in limited volume. Such craftsmen may ultimately be designing for industry or may develop their own small businesses. Frequently, they use the labor of the artisan craftsmen to follow their designs. In many regions the traditional craftsmen are divided into two categories: folk craftsmen who repeat the designs and techniques developed by their predecessors and produce for their own or neighboring communities, and those, particularly in the Orient, who still maintain the court traditions and produce objects of high and luxurious quality for use and ritual.

All have one common need—to sell their work! This creates vast complications. In the past, when markets were local, when life ran on a slow and even tempo and there were no machines, no planes or cars, no buyers from overseas, the problems were comparatively simple. Now they are deeply complex. This explains the need for the international organization of the World Crafts Council. Founded in 1964, with fifty-four countries as members, the World Crafts Council was accepted as a non-governmental member of UNESCO in 1965.

Through publications, such as this book; through biennial worldwide conferences; through a widespread information service; and by close relations with other international organizations, the Council can do much towards building greater understanding between peoples, maintaining standards of excellence, developing cooperatives and markets, and preventing the exploitation of the small craftsmen who cannot protect themselves.

It is a privilege to have been associated in the preparation of this book with Mrs. Rose Slivka, without whose untiring efforts the book could not have been assembled; to thank Mrs. Margaret M. Patch, whose knowledge of the international craft scene and wise counsel have been of enormous help; and, of course, to acknowledge the debt to our publisher, Mr. Ben Raeburn of Horizon Press, without whose vast publishing knowledge and close cooperation there would have been no book at all.

We trust the book will fill a real need—that of informing the public of the craftsmen of the modern world.

THE PERSISTENT OBJECT

by Rose Slivka

The persistent object that demands to be made whether or not society has any practical (as distinguished from real) use for it and the action men bring to this—recalling their past, renewing it in the present, investing it with the power of objective presence, whether the object be a pot or a poem —is a reality of concrete value. Expensive, long-lasting, or precious materials are not part of this value. The raku ware of the Zen tea masters draws us into its spiritual orbit to this very day. The object truly made for itself has the power to renew itself in the energies and actions of men.

Craft is the act of attention with which the craftsman brings his body rhythm to the manipulable materials of his choice. The object of craft sustains the reality of human rhythms and being. This is the essential nature of the pure object, its function and art, in its true and—in a world accelerated past the body-beat—most contemporary sense.

The basic function of craft is implicit in its original Saxon form *kraft*, meaning power and strength. The craftsman, a man of eminence, made objects to emanate and invoke power and magic (the amulet, the talisman, the charm) and invested all tools of utility with this presence—an art of symbol and inscription for protecting and extending life both in this world and the hereafter. All objects were symbols of power no less than utility; it was not until money replaced objects as the symbol of and means to power that the craftsman lost his eminence and the object was dominated by the functionalist aesthetics of the machine.

Jewelry is the exception that proves the point. Rooted in the magic power of the amulet and the talisman, while reflecting economic and social changes, it has managed to retain its basic reality in contrast to the declining power of the utilitarian crafts.

When power came to mean authority, and authority was associated with money and its artifacts of luxury, objects of jewelry became the emblems of the authority of the kings and the popes—the ring, the crown, the scepter—and the social signs of honor, distinction and wealth. Adornment continued its ancient powers in a new economic context. Still an art of symbol today, it imparts a sense of ritual enhancement, an extension of the reality of the self.

The contemporary craftsman is less directly designing for function —the reality of machine-made commodities—as he is obsessed by the nature of his materials, the interaction of the materials and himself, and the degree to which he can reach object-ness.

In his struggle to make ethical connections with his object, the craftsman of our time is making new demands on his knowledge, cultural sources, sensibilities, and experience. He is trying to create not necessarily new objects but new attitudes towards objects, to reinvest the object with its original, intrinsic reality, value, power.

The craftsman of the modern world has created an entirely unprecedented situation—a prolific and vigorous handcraft culture within the structure of industrial power. He is the paradoxical expression of an abundant society's resistance to the homogenizing pressures exerted by mass production, and of its drive to humanize and individualize, accelerated and matured through the internationalizing forces of communication.

Crafts which functioned in the communal or regional culture of an agrarian society do not have the same meaning in the internationalized culture of an industrial society. A decisive change in the nature of craft production took place when the craftsman began to create for an anonymous market, in distinct contrast to his original practice in the intimate and stable community for which he had produced. The village cabinetmaker knew the family for whom he made the chest. His forebears knew theirs and his children knew their children. He knew their specific needs and the objects the chest was intended for, and he made it to last several lifetimes, to be handed down from one generation to the next in rooted continuity and a sense of place. As the need and opportunities for mobility increased and the young dispersed, including the craftsman himself, communication took place through mechanical and electronic intermediaries bridging massive distances and populace. The unknown and perhaps unknowable consumer was somewhere out there. Furthermore, as soon as the craftsman was removed by the machine from the primary obligation of satisfying the functional needs of his market, his choice to be an object-maker became a conscious, gratuitous act. It changed the face of handcraft and signaled the beginning of a whole new creative life. The first purpose of the craftsman then was to please himself and his need was to give to the object its intrinsic material self.

In the isolation of his studio or workshop, the craftsman began to make objects that related to himself, on a scale that related to his own body in that specific space, and in materials on which he could impose his own reality or be surprised by theirs on him. He produced objects that contained his ideas (the container contained by its irrepressible, irresistible idea) and his feeling about all the objects that had ever been made in the material of his choice—clay or wood or fiber or metal—by varying cultures of his own time and those of the past.

The craftsman knows the power of objects, their omnipresence in the landscape of man. For the artist-craftsman the point of reference for whatever he makes is the object. Just as sculpture is about sculpture and painting is about painting (the figure or the landscape or the object as a means), so is the pot about pottery and all the pots that have ever been made, glass about glass, weaving about weaving, stitchery about itself, etc.

The post World War II economy of abundance and its cultural largesse of experimentation with materials and form—form which frequently these days regards function as that old skeleton in the closet—also generates an art of its omnipresent by-products: obsolescence and waste. It is the nature of the craftsman to be involved with the actual materials of his world. The sheer diversity of the discarded has captured his eye, and compelled him to invest it with new life-giving values.

Once obsolescence has given the object the patina of time and isolation from its former life, its actual values are clear. As the British architect Cedric Price points out, "The controlled structural life of an air-house contrasts with the infinite life intended for the Great Pyramid." Today, we see the calculable life of a work of art incorporated into itself as an aesthetic.

The machine has given us so many products for every conceivable purpose in every possible material—plastic, paper, glass, ceramic, fiber, metal—with such quick obsolescence that in their unremembered anonymity they make almost no demands on our sensibilities, leaving us free— easy come, easy go—from being possessed by possession.

Today, the craftsman finds himself in the quixotic position of producing more objects for a society that already has more objects than it knows what to do with.

In a world staggered by the weight and scope of its own material proliferation, we have now developed a positive culture of obsolescence. Our aesthetic values have shifted away from the traditional importances of permanence, foreverness, stability of materials and subject matter. (The artist himself, in fact, is quite aware of the imminent possibility of his own quick obsolescence as new ideas, new methods, new actions and reactions take place with such rapidity, and on an international scale, over and over again within his own lifetime.)

We no longer require ourselves to ascribe lasting values to any object —particularly functional ones. Our functional values too are changing values dictated by the artifacts and extraordinary possibilities of electronic and nuclear energies, new materials, mobility, time.

The machine proved that even a poorly made thing may function very well while it lasts; quick obsolescence has nothing to do with the ability to function. In fact, obsolescence may even reveal its aesthetic quality, like the graphic stamina of yesterday's newspaper.

Craftsmen serving purely functional purposes must be specialists of the many-faceted machine which, after all, is their all-embracing and consuming tool of production. The skill and knowledge of the mechanical engineer, the tool and dye maker, the riveter, the auto mechanic, the mold maker, is formidable. But it serves to emphasize the difference between those who serve the machine for endless production to satisfy manifold functional needs and those whom the machine serves to satisfy gratuitous needs. As a heretic against the tyranny of the machine—creating more functions for more products to satisfy its ever-increasing appetite for more production if only to keep the machines going—the artist-craftsman is free to decide whether his object is to function superbly or poorly or not at all. In so doing, he has invented a fresh new language of craft and in probing at the limits of its expression he has expanded the materials and vocabulary of art.

In the world today, in addition to the identified craft style of the designer and the highly personal craft of the artist, the third aspect of craftsmanship, the anonymous work of the folk—the unself-conscious communal expression of use and ritual—is generally disappearing with the passing of regionalism. (Where the folk craftsman is strongly individual, he transcends the rules and becomes an artist-craftsman with an identity of his own.)

In Africa and the Orient, as well as sections of Europe and Latin America, where the agrarian economy, the tribal structure, the isolation of village life, are in transition due to industrialization and international communication, the deterioration of folk handcrafts in these countries is a symptom of these changes. Secure in its affluence, the industrial west mourns for the good old days of native innocence before the corruption of money, roads, electricity, airplanes, refrigerators, telephones—before the gift of craft was converted to production for trade and export to a land the craftsman had never seen, for sale to people he would never meet, for uses he never imagined. The look of cultural nostalgia without content, without quality, without reference to the contemporaneous realities of the society that produces it, will ultimately have little meaning to a market that is itself the master of repetitive production. On the other hand, folk craft that is still untainted by "foreign" influence or trade—where the hand is still the primary method of production—can be the symptom of static culture, of isolation and poverty and ignorance.

The dominant culture of the west is an urban one with its resulting fragmentation of experience and space, united by speed on land and in the air, by telephone, radio and TV, by newspapers, magazines, books, with increasing dependence (why not?) on mechanical contrivances for every possible function. The craftsman has grasped the international experience —mobility of body and senses—as the most inevitable and galvanizing of our time.

Contrast between the industrial cultures—Europe and the U.S.A.— specifically reveals the complex directions of the artist-craftsman of the west today.

After three hundred years of trading on her greatest commodity— the culture of Renaissance humanism—about twenty years ago, post World War II Europe began to feel the twinge of diminishing returns from a restless, estranged world. Time, so long her ally, suddenly proved inconstant. The present, alas, was no longer an attribute of the past, and the past, with all its classical certainties and rich barbarism, had little to offer an industrialized world blind enough to build atomic fortresses on the eroding edges of the sky. Her thinking artists and designers had long known she could not go on being a monument to her past and, beginning with the early part of this century, they fought with formidable success the intellectual battle for the magnetism of the present against the weight of the past.

Heavily laden with a craft and design consciousness (one that has been a great influence even in painting and sculpture), and a continent full of artisans trained to performance, Europe underwent the painful process of re-evaluating creative work in every field. The European craftsman-designer, traditional standard-bearer of the artifacts of humanism, once more reaffirmed its presence in a still human world with a body of new work—new designs of superb contemporary grace, notably from Italy and Scandinavia. The intellectual doldrums of fascism, the devastation of World War II, the deep conflicts in postwar values—all this could not diminish the tenacious spirit of the European craftsman and designer.

Until only one hundred years ago, the development of regional crafts was fostered by dukes and kings who ruled independent principalities in a competitive display of wealth and power. So different were—and still are —the styles, the work, the temperaments of the people, and the tempo of life of the different regions that the only generalization one can make is on the prevailing love of craftsmanship as such. With the apprenticeship system still the educational mainstay of every trade, the tradition for perfection in labor has been communicated even to the machine worker. The best of the creative craftsmen are employed by their own home market. Beauty-loving and craft-conscious consumers are their active patrons. That designer-craftsmen work actively and sympathetically with architects, and also do industrial and graphic design, gives further testimony to their solid status in contemporary European life.

In the U.S.A., by contrast, the craftsman never did produce for a ruling hierarchy, and only for a very short time for his immediate agricultural community before he was rendered unnecessary by the Industrial Revolution.

As in the other arts, U.S. crafts also have broken new ground and challenged past traditions, suggested new meanings and possibilities to old functions and habits of seeing. What are the factors in the historical and philosophic fabric of America that engendered the mood of their expression?

The U.S.A.—compelled by the electrifying and still new idea of personal freedom that cut through geographic, social and economic lines to impel people everywhere in unparalleled scope and numbers—was the economic spawn of the Industrial Revolution. In the three hundred years of their short history, their expanding frontier kept them absorbed in the problems of practical function and pressured them to solve them in a hurry. They have, as a result, developed a national style in satisfying functional needs for the mass in a massive country, with availability an ideal.

Not unified by blood or national origin—everyone is from some place else—or a sense of place (with many generations of a family history identified with one place), as in Europe, the Orient and Africa, they are a restless people. A nation of immigrants with a continuing history of migration, they are obsessed by the need for arrival—a pursuit whose goal eludes them; so they are always on the go. (Their writers—Walt Whitman, Herman Melville, Thomas Wolfe—have repeatedly explored this theme.) Having solved their need for mobility by mechanical means, they love engineering and performance and the materials and tools by which they have achieved them. If there is any one pervasive element in the American climate, it is that of the machine—its energy, its productivity, its violence.

In their involvement with practical matters, they were too busy really to cultivate the idea of beauty. Beauty as such may not be the aesthetic impetus in an American scene, a scene which has been infused not only with the dynamics of machine technology, but with the action of men—ruggedly individual and vernacular men (the pioneer, the cowboy), with a genius for improvisation. Their environment, temperament, creative tensions do not seem to encourage the making of beauty, but rather the act of beauty as creative adventure—energy at work—tools and materials finding each other—machines in movement—power and speed—always incomplete, always in process.

Nothing is needed to last forever, and the rough-and-tumble of U.S. craft, which considers the expressive content most important and takes great liberties with the material, is in distinct contrast to the thrifty, careful, and even cautious practice in other parts of the world where predetermined modes of traditional design guard against waste, where exquisitely exacting and nonwasteful techniques have been invented and evolved with the minimum of materials and tools, where materials are precious and labor is plentiful.

The **freedom** of the American craftsman to experiment, to risk, to make mistakes freely on a creative and quantitative level has been facilitated to a large extent by the wealth of tools and materials. It gives further impetus to the craftsman's involvement in total process—in the mastery of technology and the actual making of the object from beginning to end —in marked contrast to the artist-craftsmen of other countries who do only the designing and finishing and leave the technology and execution to the peasant craftsman. Aside from the fact that there is in the U.S. no anonymous peasant craftsman to do only the technical or preparatory work, the craftsman loves his tools too much to leave that part of the fun to someone else. For him the entire process contains creative possibilities. Intimacy with the tools and materials of his craft is a source of the artist's power. Here too, however, lies a contradiction.

In the U.S., since there is no folk art tradition, except in some Indian communities too often sealed off from their non-Indian neighbors, to learn about a craft one must go to an art school or a university where, frequently, the reward of technique is its own virtue. This has been accompanied by rebellion against the tyranny of traditional techniques (after having learned them), by deliberate rejection of customary tools, processes and materials among artists who break every rule. This ambivalence toward technique is a characteristic of the modern craftsman.

The American craftsman, then, is an intellectual, the product of the university workshop or specialized school with study in painting and sculpture as well as design and craft techniques. Having turned to the craft heritage of the rest of the world for lack of an indigenous one, he has had to study. Instead of learning his techniques from the folk craftsman or through heritage or apprenticeship, he does his research in books, in the workshops of universities and by traveling to countries with a craft tradition. The craftsman of the U.S. is the product of international experience. He is, furthermore, a veritable melting pot of national origins, with the professional artist-craftsmen who emigrated from Europe and the Orient as the decisive influences.

All over the western world the objects of the new object-makers provide moral and ethical confrontation with a society that has become alienated from its objects, that no longer accepts responsibility for them, is unable to see them, uses them mechanically. The object-makers are commenting on their middle-class culture of mass-produced, standardized good taste as a domesticated, house-broken, sanitized sensibility. They make no aesthetic conclusion. The objects are their own comment, their own mute drama. They accuse, they amuse, they challenge. Having shed their roles as functional or decorative intermediaries, they assume their own objective aspect, and we are brought face to face with the heightened concrete perception.

Identity induced by words separates things from themselves. Things lose their power and become illustrations of the word which, when it ceased to be hieroglyph, or pictographic representation of the object, ceased actual connection with the thing and became its own abstract and powerful object. While seeking the connection between objects, person, and language, the object-makers create a mutual absoluteness for each. The perspective is one of the surreal space of interacting isolation—of stillness, of object, of person, of space, of word.

On the other hand, surrounded by a word-filled world dominated by publication and publicity, our process of education glibly teaches us the vocabulary and the reproduction before we know the actual object. We see objects through synthetic media—books, magazines, television, movies. We see them (maybe) in transition, as we walk from one place to the next, in the speed of our cars, planes, etc. Actual confrontation in time and space is rare.

The young artist has also found that he cannot trust the inside of things—the heart stops beating, the TV tube burns out—which he cannot see and which, in any case, look quite different from the outside form and are suspect, therefore, on still another count. In the objects he makes, everything is exteriorized, all surface, totally visible all at once. It does what you see and you see what it does. There is no mystery, no enigma, no inner life, no conflict. All is cool.

While the symbols of American life continue to excite creative craftsmen abroad, the European, Oriental and African craft traditions continue to enrich the American craftsman. This is further underscored by the fact that more than 25,000 students from the U.S. are studying abroad, while over 100,000 students from all over the world are studying in the universities of the U.S.A. Craftsmen everywhere, including the humble, anonymous member of a cottage industry whose work is known for its traditional national mode, are members of the modern, international milieu into which each artist reaches out to expand his own unique and individual gamut. While American designers may use the old motifs of Nigeria, the colors of India, the textures of Japan, Nigerian craftsmen are in turn using such modern motifs of industrial society as cement intaglio reliefs of bulldozers, planes and cranes on their buildings. The craftsmen of San Blas Islands produce the most exquisitely appliquéd blouses decorated with images of Superman and Donald Duck. And so it goes.

This book—a pictorial compendium of over four hundred objects of contemporary craft from some seventy countries—shows the live, multifaceted presence of the handcraftsman in the modern world. We regret the exclusion of many craftsmen of stature equal to those here included and necessarily omitted for lack of space or other technical considerations. We also regret that all the craft media could not be represented for each country in which they are practiced. This survey, however, while necessarily incomplete, is intended to suggest the vigor and variety of stylistic directions, diversity in materials, exciting mutations and hybridizations taking place in crafts today—from the functional to the functionless, from the traditional to the experimental, from the aesthetic to the anti-aesthetic, from the unified to the fragmented—pushing the traditional confines into whole new areas of creative power.

All work shown is current as we go to press. New work is being done with fresh creative insight by artists we have yet to hear about, as well as those we know. The story, happily, is an ever-continuing, incompletable and changing one.

In a culture of mass education by mass graphic and electronic reproduction, we are bound to create and perpetuate myths which in turn give rise to other realities. A photograph is a tonal reinterpretation on paper of the object that actually exists in the world. A photograph is not itself the object. There are bad things that can look great in photographs and good things that look weak because they are unphotographable. Creating craft and seeing craft are not the same. Writing about craft is not the same as making it. There is no substitution for confrontation with the actual object.

This selection was culled from over ten thousand photographs. Final choices were made on the basis of photographic quality and the graphic design requirements of the book itself within the space available. Succeeding publications, we hope, will investigate the crafts of each area in greater depth.

Throughout their long history, crafts have produced useful objects which are later considered fine art. Time has a way of overwhelming the functional values of an object that outlives the men who made and used it, with the power of its own objective presence—that life-invested quality of being that transcends and energizes. When this happens, such objects are forever honored for their own sakes—they are art.

As a lover of reality and its materials in action and object, the craftsman has crossed lines not only internationally and between the fine arts and the crafts, but also between them and the theater, poetry, film, music—all aesthetic values in performance and thinking today.

The handcraftsman—utterly surrounded by the magnitude of an automated technology that can not only destroy the world he lives in but create another at the push of a button; where the most powerful forces of our environment—electronic and atomic, inner and outer space, speed—are invisible to the naked eye; living in a world which lacks status in the universe and like a diminutive Ping-Pong ball bounces around with other little planets under one of many possible suns—is expressing the dilemma of all men in our time. The aspect of man is no longer the center of things and his eyes are only accessories of his own growing sense of displacement. In the face of all this, the survival of the handcraftsman—enemy of mechanical mindlessness—carrying the weight of humanism with all its objects of art and utility that define it as a culture—testifies to the persistence of man's exuberant reverence of himself, of man the artist, the lover of life, his own best reason for being.

by Margaret Merwin Patch

○ ASIA   It is logical to start this survey with Asia, a continent whose long cultural history is fully documented by its crafts.

Craftsmen from time immemorial have supplied the skilled labor for this vast continent. Working in family groups or in small workshops, they have provided articles for household and other local needs, for trade, and for requirements of courts and temples.

The craftsman who designs and makes his own products, and who exhibits and sells under his own name, is relatively unknown in Asia, except in Japan. A few individual craftsmen who have been trained in other countries have achieved critical acclaim, but this only emphasizes the anonymity of craftsmen in general.

Historically, the status of craftsmen in Japan has always been high. The traditional craftsmen who create articles for use in the ritual tea ceremony and for the family shrine are still rewarded with honor and, often, with very high prices. Known as "art crafts," these articles are sold with the signature of the grand master; no copies are made.

JAPAN Such articles, together with such other traditional craft work as ceremonial brocades, embroidered kimonos, and fine lacquer ware are shown in the semi-official "traditional crafts" exhibitions sponsored by the Ministry of Education. Many of the older craftsmen who have done especially fine work are given the title of "Living National Treasure" by the Japanese government, together with a pension. This is a distinction which has no counterpart in any other nation.

Another current in Japanese crafts has been the folk art movement (Mingei), started about thirty years ago to emulate the simplicity and honesty of the folk arts and the "beauty of anonymity." Through the travels and lectures of its founders, and exhibitions of their work, this group has achieved world renown. It has exerted much influence, especially in pottery. Many of the pottery villages have become famous, Mashiko, Bizen, Nagoya and Tachikui, to name a few.

One of the newer groups is that of the young industrial artists, which recognizes the importance of proper selling. Their products are displayed not only at their own showcase in Tokyo, Craft Center Japan, but in the good design corners in department stores of that city. Their chief organization is the Japan Designer Craftsmen Association; included in this are also the young industrial designers, an overlapping group.

An important recent influence on the crafts of

The material for this section was gathered by travel to over fifty countries by questionnaire and by the questioning of the many visitors from all parts of the world at the offices of the World Crafts Council. It has been prepared to offer to students and travelers as much source information as possible in the limited space. The English translation of the native words has been generally used.

Japan has been that of architects and interior designers, who increasingly employ well-known craftsmen to ornament and furnish the new buildings, with ceramic and carved wall decoration, furniture, carpets and hangings. Increasingly international in outlook, Japanese craftsmen seek entry in international seminars and exhibitions, and recently formed two associations to draw foreign exhibitors to Japan— the International Ceramics Association, and the Japanese Contemporary Craftsmen's Association.

Many famous traditional craftsmen are in Kyoto, the old capital, long a center of the arts. Also in Kyoto are found many of the young experimental artist-craftsmen, notably the So-dei-sha ceramics group, whose leader has recently exhibited as a sculptor. Apprentice systems still operate effectively in the villages. More advanced education in the crafts is offered by art schools and university art departments, most of them in Tokyo. Craft exhibitions are held occasionally in the Museum of Modern Art in Tokyo and to some extent in private galleries, but more often in the exhibition halls of the big department stores, a uniquely Japanese phenomenon.

The important Japanese craft media are ceramics, textiles, wood, lacquer, metal and bamboo.

The craft situation in Korea is much like that in   KOREA Japan, especially in that the crafts are similar and that there is the same high regard for education. Three colleges in Seoul offer four-year courses in ceramics, silk screen printing, enamelling, weaving, wood carving, and leatherwork. There are twelve junior colleges with two-year courses. Exhibitions of the work of single individuals are rare, but group exhibitions sponsored by the government or the various universities occur as often as ten times a year in the capital city of Seoul.

The traditional crafts of both Hong Kong and Tai- HONG KONG wan reflect those of mainland China: carved teak   TAIWAN and camphor wood furniture, carpets and rugs, pewter and brassware, ivory and jade carving, gold jewelry, masks, articles of wood and rattan, lacquer ware, lanterns, and other paper articles.

In Hong Kong the skills of Chinese craftsmen, many of them refugees, are being utilized in efficient workshops producing a wide variety of products for export.

On Taiwan, the influx of craftsmen from the mainland has given new impetus to the local handcraft industry, and the Handicraft Promotion Center encourages production for sale to tourists and for export. A permanent handicraft showroom is maintained to introduce good design to the public, and to encourage producers.

Much has been done in the Philippines to revive, PHILIPPINES develop and improve existing crafts and to introduce new ones. Schools, social and civic groups, government agencies, and foreign aid have offered substantial assistance for the promotion of cottage industries. The most important organization is the National Cottage Industries Development Authority.

In addition to the basic craft media, the work of craftsmen in the Philippines includes grass weaving and basketry, rattan and shell work.

INDONESIA On Java, a principal craft area is the former capital of Djokjakarta, which is also the headquarters of the Division of Art Education of the Ministry of Education and Culture, and its Akademi Seni Rupa, (Academy of Fine Arts). In the Batik Institute, painting with drops of wax is done by girls; the pattern printing with an iron-pronged instrument dipped into the wax, by the men. Ceremonial silver bowls and coffee services are made in nearby Kota Gede.

Of special interest on the island of Bali are the traditional dancers, whose influence on the crafts inspires the rich costumes, headdresses and masks, and also, the musical instruments. Here, one finds also the religious shadow play, with its mythological figures carved from water buffalo hide in lacy fineness. Bali is the center of a well organized group of craftsmen, perhaps the best known of whom are the wood carvers at Mas.

MALAYSIA Most of the surviving Malaysian crafts are produced with assistance from the government organization, MARA, formerly the Rural and Industrial Development Authority. These are sold in Kuala Lumpur, mainly at the government-run Malay Handicrafts Shop.

CAMBODIA Formerly part of French Indochina, Cambodia still shows some French influence in the Ecole des Beaux Arts, under the Department of Education in Pnom Penh. Taught there are painting, drawing, sculpture, wood carving, gold and silver work, enamelling, metal casting and weaving. All designs are traditional, however, with Buddhist symbols in evidence, especially the venerated Naga (cobra) on the embossed silver work.

VIETNAM With strong government support, craft activity is centered in the Handicraft Center, a former French department store on the main shopping street of Saigon. The principal modern crafts sold here are pottery, weaving, silk screen printing, lacquer, tortoise shell products and woven straw products.

THAILAND Crafts have flourished in Bangkok as the city has become one of the main stops on the international tourist route. Its streets are lined with shops selling a variety of crafts, notably the Thai silks, now in demand in the fashion centers of Europe and America.

The craft production centers of Thailand are in the Bangkok-Thonburi section, and at Chiengmai in the north with nearby silver, paper and weaving villages, and the factory where celadon pottery is being revived.

In the southern provinces metal work predominates: silver, gold, niello, bronze; also textiles and batik. At Ubol, near the Cambodian border, intricately woven ikat silks cost little more than the glowing, solid colors. In the silver villages, bowls are raised by men squatting over their ground forges, and then are embossed perfectly by the women, free-hand.

At the University of Fine Arts in Bangkok, an awareness of contemporary crafts has recently emerged; at Chulalongkorn University courses in industrial design, weaving, and ceramics have been established, taught by craftsmen educated abroad.

BURMA Rangoon is the center of government activities in behalf of the crafts, but to see craftsmen at work one must go to outlying areas, such as Mandalay, long a center of arts and culture, the metal village of Saigain, whose bowls are still embossed in designs from the story of the *Ramayana*, and the silk-weaving village of Amarapura with its gauzes. The lacquer industry of Pagan uses the same split bamboo base as is found at Chiengmai, close across the border in Thailand.

The School of Fine Arts in Rangoon which is government supported has a planned program including painting, sculpture, clay modeling, bronze casting, wood carving, stone carving, silver work and weaving.

To encourage the crafts, the government of India **INDIA** has promoted cooperative financing of long-term credit for the purchase of equipment and materials, and cooperative selling of the product. Still in process is a detailed census of craftsmen, by localities and by crafts, which will provide a basis for future planning. The work of the All India Handicraft Board has been so successful that its leaders are often consulted by other countries.

By far the most important craft is weaving in many traditional techniques. According to an official estimate there are two million hand looms and six million persons involved in the textile industry. Most of the traditional fabrics can be seen in the Central Cottage Industries Emporium in New Delhi. There one finds the celebrated silk and gold brocade saris from Benares; the embroidered Kashmir shawls, and the famous shatoosh of such fineness that they can be drawn through a ring; the tie-dye scarfs and saris from Jaipur; the block prints on cotton from Sanganer; the embroidery in all its variety, often embellished with beads or bits of mirror; the applique work; the painted temple cloths; the coarse handspun khadi associated with Gandhi. Other traditional crafts include jewelry of gold, silver, and enamel; silver on brass repousse from Tanjore; Bidri work, papier mache, lacquered wood; carved stone, the newly revived blue ceramic ware; and sandlewood and ivory carvings.

It is still possible to see many traditional crafts in their native setting: go to Benares, where ornamental metal utensils are used for ritual bathing in the Ganges River; to the annual cloth fair at Madras; to see the magnificent heavy jewelry of the hill tribes; to see the village ceramists making the huge grain storage pots, often five feet high, or the large terra cotta horses which symbolically guard a village. Or, one may see the women winding thread to make the hundreds of dots in the pattern of a tie-dye sari, working in their indigo-splashed quarters in Jaipur or Tiruchirappalli.

Since these arts are taught by apprenticeship, little formal training for the crafts is available. A very few art schools offer craft courses: among them are the Government College of Arts and Crafts in Calcutta and the Sir J. J. School of Art in Bombay. Recently a new Design Institute opened at Ahmedabad. In general, in the teaching of crafts the emphasis is almost entirely on techniques and on traditional design. Exception is found in the trade schools and workshops of the Regional Design Centers of the All India Handicraft Board and All India Handloom Board, where there is continual experimentation with design.

In only a very few cases have individual craftsmen been invited to exhibit their work as artists at the All India Fine Arts and Crafts Society. Regional exhibits are beginning to be held, and the Craft Museum of the All India Handicraft Board in New Delhi exhibits both old and modern work. However, traditional village craft work continues to be largely anonymous.

With a strong sense of their cultural importance, the government supports craft publications to be sent abroad, and often sends craft emissaries of distinction to other countries. In addition to the government agencies, the Indian Crafts Council, with branches in the various states, promotes the purely cultural aspects of the handcrafts.

NEPAL Nepal has always been rich in crafts, which today include traditional weaving, embroidery, masks, metal work, wood carving of figures, and decorative objects studded often with coral, turquoise and other semiprecious stones. A Tibetan relief organization produces pile rugs in traditional colors and patterns.

SIKKIM In Sikkim the crafts include carpets, woodwork, gold and silver work, dolls, boot and hat making, batiks, and handmade paper. In both countries there are cottage and small industry groups sponsored by the governments.

CEYLON Recently, effort has been made to foster the folk arts by various agencies, with liaison between headquarters and shops in Colombo and workers in various parts of the country.

Singhalese craft media include metal, pottery, textiles, wood, coconut shells, mats of ekel lace, ebony and ivory carving, brassware and silver filigree.

PAKISTAN As in India, weaving is first in importance among the crafts. In Karachi, all kinds of work is done, as craftsmen have moved there to be near their markets; of note there is a contemporary block printing workshop. Lahore is another traditional craft area, with woodwork, weaving and embroidery. Brass and copper products are found mostly around Peshawar; pottery and tiles in the Sind Desert and East Pakistan. In Dacca in East Pakistan is found very fine weaving of cotton and silk; in Chittagong, wood, mats and baskets; in Hala, wood, enamels, pottery and weaving. Other crafts include jewelry, lacquer, inlaid wood, leatherwork, and glass.

Organizations concerned with the crafts include the Pakistan Small Industries Development Center, with design and display centers in Karachi and Lahore and the All Pakistan Women's Association, APWA, with its own shops. At Lahore, the National College of Arts offers courses in furniture and product design, ceramics; textiles printing, including wood block, silk screen and batik; wrought iron, copper, brass and white metal work.

AFGHANISTAN In the Small Industries Display Center in Kabul are shown works of indigenous origin and those of more recent design. Among the important crafts are the finely knotted carpets, including Bokhara rugs; embroidery, weaving, block printing, and metal work.

IRAN The brocades and cut velvet and gold cloth of Persia have long been famous, known even in the early courts of Europe. Persian carpets are museum treasures the world around. Tiles covering the mosques are masterpieces of architectural decoration, while the designs on the pottery, which go back to 6000 B.C., are among the oldest paintings of mankind. There is still much hand production throughout the country, notably in Isfahan, Tabriz, Mamedan, Meched and Yezd.

Within the Ministry of Economy, a Centre for Small Scale Industry and Handicrafts has been established to safeguard and expand the crafts produced in workshops or in homes. Under the Fine Arts Department of the Ministry of Education, an institute with an adjoining Folklore Arts Museum has been set up in Tehran to preserve the best of the ancient crafts. Seen here are knotted Persian rugs; etched brass and copper trays and hollow ware; silk brocades and cut velvet; repousse silver work; jewelry, and enamelling; ceramics, including ornamental tiles; wood inlay, and furniture; hand-woven fabrics of silk, wool and cotton; embroidery and other fabric ornamentation.

IRAQ A Directorate of Popular Culture and Crafts works to preserve ancient traditions, and in the Ministry of Education is an Institute of Fine Arts whose aims supplement those of the Directorate.

In the south are found matting, rope making, and boat construction from palm trees and reeds; in the north, stone carving and wooden articles. The centuries-old filigree is made by the Sabean community. Other craft products are pottery, tiles, mosaics, brocades, printed and woven fabrics, copper pots, jewelry, knotted carpets, goat hair rugs, and leather work.

SYRIA Syria is still a thriving craft country, producing articles for sale all over the eastern Mediterranean area. Many of the busy workshops are in Damascus and Aleppo, but much work is also produced in villages throughout the country. All the craft work consists of skillful copying of traditional designs.

A wide variety of crafts is made: carpets and rugs; brass and copper, hammered, enamelled and inlaid; furniture, carved or inlaid with ivory, mother of pearl; mosaics.

The Syrian government is much concerned with handcrafts, and exerts leadership through the Director of Rural Industry of the Ministry of Social Affairs. A central training workshop in Damascus gives intensive training to village craft leaders. Also in Damascus are two women's organizations which furnish materials for home embroidery work.

LEBANON Lebanon was formerly a part of Syria and still imports from that country most of the crafts sold in the local markets. A few notable exceptions are the pictorial silk tapestries of Zouk, and the Jezzine tableware of silver and horn. A bell-casting plant in Beit Chabab village sends church bells to many countries. Fine embroidery is taught and produced in the Roman Catholic convents near Beirut. The American University of Beirut expects to introduce courses in crafts in the art department.

JORDAN Apart from the indigenous crafts, made and used by the people of the country, the principal crafts are the weaving of cotton cloth from thread dyed in Damascus; cross-stitch embroidery; Bedouin rugs woven of sheep's wool and of camels' hair, notably from Tafila and Kerak. The mother-of-pearl works at Bethlehem, the glassblowing establishment at Hebron, and the modern pottery in East Jerusalem are notable.

ISRAEL In Israel there is considerable interest in preserving traditional crafts, in developing contemporary crafts, and in designing for industry. Over five hundred craftsmen are known by name. The principal media are ceramics; weaving and tapestries, textile printing; wood turning and carving; glassblowing; brass and copper work; jewelry, and other silver and gold work; enamelling and furniture.

The ministries most interested in crafts are Education, Labor, and Commerce and Industry; Maskit Development of Home Industries Company, with shops in eight cities, is a government organization which promotes and develops home crafts among new immigrants.

The major craft school in Israel is the Bezalel School in Jerusalem, which gives four years of academy-level training in weaving, graphics, silver and metal ware, painting, sculpture and ceramics. There are also a number of schools at the secondary level and two major handcraft centers of the Kibbutz organization. Seminars for handcraft teaching are conducted by the Ministry of Education and Culture and the Ministry of Labor.

TURKEY The crafts include work in iron, copper, brass and silver; enamels and jewelry; knotted carpets, kilims and embroidered rugs; alabaster, amber and meerschaum carving; weaving, embroidery, knitting, and lace making; ceramics, including glazed and hand-painted ware, kutahya peasant ware, and terra cotta incised in the Hittite tradition.

Crafts come under the direction of a number of government departments, from the Ministry of Education to the Small Industries Department of the Department of Labor, and a number of private organizations, especially the Association for Promoting Turkish Handicrafts, all in Ankara. The Union of Chambers of Commerce and Industry and also the Travel Association of Turkey are concerned with the production of crafts for the tourist industry. Courses in textiles and ceramics are given at the Istanbul Academy of Fine Arts and in embroidery and sewing at the Girls' Technical Institutes in Ankara and Istanbul. Trade courses in fabric and rug weaving are given in twenty-six cities.

There are a number of artist-craftsmen, especially in ceramics.

O EUROPE In general, the emergence of the creative craftsman and the development of contemporary crafts has been best supported in the northern countries, where for many decades there have been strong craft organizations. Especially in the Scandinavian countries, the cooperative associations of arts and industrial design have been a powerful worldwide influence on design. An important recent development has been the support of crafts in the socialist countries of eastern Europe, most notably Czechoslovakia.

The continued eminence of European design is due not only to the tradition of high style in European capitals, but also the generally high level of art education: the arts and crafts schools of Europe are many and influential, the training in fundamentals is stressed—often beginning in the secondary schools—and many "high schools" of arts and crafts offer comprehensive courses leading to a degree. A special feature of the European craft scene, has long been the trade fairs, where products of the handcraft industries are shown along with machinery and other industrial products. Notable also are the craft and design publications in a number of European countries, such as Sweden, Germany, Switzerland and Italy.

YUGOSLAVIA Contributing to the revitalization of applied arts have been the Academy of Art in Belgrade and nine secondary schools, and the applied arts museums in Belgrade and Zagreb, both of which show modern crafts. More and more, applied arts are assuming the character of modern art, and Yugoslav craftsmen have received recognition at home and abroad in the areas of textiles, metals, and ceramics.

The Federation of Artists of Applied Arts, with affiliated societies in the six republics, has over eight hundred members; it includes not only crafts, but dress design, graphic design, display, interior design, product and engineering design, art photography, film and theatre design. Its aim is the improvement of crafts and design as indispensable factors in the craft-based industries.

BULGARIA Contemporary artist-craftsmen have an association, the Union of Bulgarian Artists, whose work is displayed at the center called "Exhibit for Folklore Art."

In Rumania, as in other eastern European countries, there has been a government-directed effort to put the folk arts on a strong economic footing. The contemporary art-crafts are also recognized, with a modern shop for their sale. **RUMANIA**

The Union of Plastic Artists in Bucharest is an organization of professional artists and craftsmen which publishes an art magazine. The Museum of Popular Art displays its folk art in a discriminating contemporary manner, and in Bucharest there is also an important open-air museum of peasant homes and folk arts.

So far most of the recent craft revival has taken the form of artistic and technical assistance in the production of traditional crafts by the National Organization of Hellenic Handicrafts and by Their Majesties' Fund. There is now springing up a group of contemporary artist-craftsmen, chiefly ceramists, many of whom work at Maroussi near Athens, and a proposal has recently been made to develop an international ceramics center on the island of Sifnos. **GREECE**

Besides ceramics, characteristic crafts include two-harness weaving of cloth in bright stripes; wood carving on buildings and in household articles; handknotted carpets in Turkish style, kilims, and long-fleeced wool rugs; much embroidery used as fabric decoration and on cross stitch rugs and wall hangings; lace making, dolls in national costume, jewelry, metal work and basketry.

The Corporation of Decorative Art provides group workshops, and there are many craftsmen who work independently. A few of the outstanding crafts include ceramics, batiks, gobelin designing and weaving, embossed silver work, experimental work in glass and plastics. **HUNGARY**

There is an excellent School of Arts and Crafts in Budapest, giving a four-year advanced course in a wide variety of subjects. Professional designer-craftsmen are members of the Council of Hungarian Industrial Design and Art Crafts. In Budapest, also, there is also the Union of National Cooperatives of Folklore Handicrafts.

In Czechoslovakia, the government has seriously undertaken the saving and rebuilding of the applied arts, and in 1956 created an organization, the Center of Applied Art, to educate young craftsmen. With an office in Prague for Czech regions and one in Bratislava for Slovak regions, it has over fifty centers, managed by master craftsmen. In its sculptors' workshops are architectural workers: stonemasons, mosaicists, stucco workers, painters, metal founders and experts in the setting of stained glass windows. In other workshops are gobelin weaving, carpet-knotting, wood carving, artistic forging, chain making and hand printing on textiles. In the studios are jewelry, silversmithing, bookbinding, decoration, engraving and glass cutting. Much contemporary work is done for new building, and outstanding experimental work is done in lace and glass. **CZECHOSLOVAKIA**

The Union of Czechoslovak Creative Artists in Prague is the association of professional artists of applied arts, primarily designers, though some execute finished work. Membership is by jury and must be renewed from time to time. The union submits designs as requested by government agencies and also sells to the public through government shops.

The Museum of Applied Arts of the National Gallery shows works of modern craftsmen and designers. There is good magazine coverage of the crafts, both domestic and international.

There is strict division in Poland between the **POLAND**

24

work of artist-craftsmen and the folk arts; each is handled by a completely separate organization. The folk art division, CPLIA, has a strong marketing organization and maintains its own shops in several countries.

The important crafts of Poland are weaving, ceramics, straw braiding, paper cutouts, embroidery, smithing, furriery, wood carving and toy making. Most famous, the Polish tapestries have been shown as works of art in major art museums in many countries.

The Interior Decoration and Decorative Art Section of the Union of Polish Artists is an association of the artist-craftsmen and designers in the craft field. Several other government agencies are interested in the crafts; perhaps the one best known abroad is the Institute of Industrial Design, which has experimented with using folklore artists as designers for mass production.

U.S.S.R. The U.S.S.R. has well organized folk, amateur, and professional craft work. Craftsmen working in the traditional folk arts are organized in government workshops, each craft centered in its original area to make use of existing skilled workers as teachers. This work is under the direction of the Scientific Research Institute of Artistic Industry, which sends its designers throughout the country looking for the best examples to be copied or to be redesigned for workshop production, and for display in the Museum of Folk Art in Moscow.

Amateur artists and craftsmen are encouraged by a House of Peoples' Art in each main city, with a professional in attendance to help if needed. Work of this kind is exhibited locally, then regionally and, finally, the best is shown in Moscow every four years, with prizes and awards at each level.

Professional craftsmen work in all media. They are organized in the Union of Artists of the U.S.S.R., which publishes a magazine, and which has a special Exhibitions Division. The most important art schools are in Moscow and Leningrad.

FINLAND The status of crafts in Finland today is an enviable one. ORNAMO, the Finnish Society of Decorative Artists, encourages craftsmen and makes them known at home and abroad by arranging frequent exhibitions and competitions. There is cooperation between architects and craftsmen, and between industry and craftsmen.

The important media are glass, ceramics, woodworking, plywood sculpture, tapestries, rya rugs, printed fabrics, shawls and scarves, silversmithing, jewelry, and lighting fixtures. Crafts are taught at the Finnish Institute of Crafts and Design in Helsinki, founded by ORNAMO.

SWEDEN Swedish handcrafts, in common with those of other Scandinavian countries, enjoy wide international acceptance in sophisticated communities. Here the industrial designer, often himself a practicing craftsman, has come into his own. It is a widespread practice for an artist-designer to work for a specific factory, designing for mass-produced goods, but at the same time to have a studio at his disposal for making unique pieces. During the last decade, there has been increasing use of handcrafts in architecture, the decorative works of designer-craftsmen.

The principal crafts of Sweden are furniture making, weaving of tapestries and rugs, printing of decorative fabrics and dress materials, ceramics and glass. The principal school is the State School of Arts, Crafts and Design in Stockholm. There are several design and crafts organizations, among them the Association of Craftsmen and Industrial Designers, and the Swedish Society for Industrial Design. A permanent exhibition is maintained at the Hantverket in Stockholm, showroom for the Handicraft Guild.

Of considerable importance is the program of the Swedish Handcraft Industries Association, Hemslöjd, with the special products of the regions varying from Lapp crafts in the north to textiles of Scania in the south.

NORWAY In Norway today, designers work closely with craftsmen, there being comparatively few small workshops where the designer or craftsman personally designs and executes the product. In general, the wholly handmade object and the machine-made product are made under the same roof, the result of team work in which the aesthetic and the practical are coordinated.

The National Society of Norwegian Arts and the Crafts is allied under a general national organization with the associations of plastic artists and of architects; it coordinates the work of the associations of applied art in five regional centers. The crafts include all the principal media.

There is a central school of arts and crafts in Oslo and one in Bergen. In addition there are technical schools in various cities whose educational programs are connected with workshops; there are also special schools for training of apprentices.

DENMARK In modern times, characteristic Danish design has been a leader in metalware, furniture, weaving and ceramics. There are signs that the sharp distinctions between painter, sculptor, and handcraftsman are disappearing in a country where industry has appreciated artist, designer and craftsman equally.

Organizations of professional craftsmen are the Danish Society of Arts and Crafts and Industrial Design, and also Den Permanente, a permanent exhibition and sales organization for craftsmen and industrial designers in Copenhagen. Over the years these two organizations, with the support of an enlightened government, have sent abroad purely cultural exhibitions of the finest in Danish crafts, thereby improving Denmark's international image. The Danish Handicraft Guild is concerned with the cottage industries and includes the handcrafts of Iceland, a former Danish dependency. The Danish Institute holds an annual international study and workshop seminar for two weeks in connection with the Scandinavian Design Cavalcade, in an attempt to combine both a theoretical and a practical introduction to Danish handicraft, art, and architecture.

UNITED KINGDOM England has never specialized in any craft but covers a wide range. There has been a revival of tapestry weaving and, quite recently, a popularity in woven and knotted rugs. Pottery, possibly, comes next, with centers in Wales and, from times immemorial, in the north of England.

Other notable crafts are gold and silversmithing, woodwork and furniture making, bookbinding and calligraphy, and work in glass. In addition there are gun making, saddlery and musical instruments.

The Crafts Centre of Great Britain maintains a permanent craft exhibition, and a directory of craftsmen. The Design Centre is also concerned with crafts. Schools teaching crafts include the Royal College of Art and Goldsmiths College in London, arts and crafts schools in London, Sheffield, Birmingham, Leeds, and elsewhere. In addition, most local authorities provide training, and some firms and individual craftsmen are prepared to take apprentices.

IRELAND In the list of Irish crafts are found the traditional linens and tweeds, lace, Beleek and other pottery, bogwood carving, rush work, silver, stained glass, and the newly revived Waterford glass. The craft revival is being sponsored not only by the tourist and export departments of the government, but by the Irish Society for Design and Craftwork in Dublin.

BELGIUM
NETHERLANDS
LUXEMBOURG Contemporary handcrafts in Belgium, the Netherlands and Luxembourg, cover a wide range of media. The Netherlands has taken the lead in organization by setting up a Coordinating Committee for the Exhibition of Arts and Crafts Abroad, and the artist-craftsmen of the three countries are planning a joint effort to improve the status of the crafts.

In the Netherlands there are a number of government agencies with overlapping interests in the crafts and three associations with craftsmen-members. There are subsidized schools teaching crafts in eleven cities, where students can specialize as free artists or craftsmen, working alone or as designers in industry or architecture. Certain museums buy and show crafts in special exhibitions, especially in Amsterdam, Rotterdam, and The Hague; there is also a glass museum at Leerdam and one for ceramics at Gouda.

In Belgium, a committee including interior designers and architects as well as craftsmen has called strongly for Benelux cooperation.

GERMANY In Germany, the craftsman still occupies a strong position in the economy to which his skills make a substantial contribution. The goal for craftsmanship in Germany today is not merely to preserve the traditions in technical and artistic excellence, but also to improve design, and to create wide popular acceptance. Many of the young craftsmen are experimenting in the contemporary vein in all media, with special emphasis on wrought iron work.

The Federation of German Art-Handcrafts is a group which includes the associations of the separate states, and which receives certain government support. Notable is the state-supported triennial international exhibition at Stuttgart. The Cologne Museum of Decorative Arts has organized and sent abroad traveling exhibitions of crafts. The Munich Handicrafts and Trade Fair and the Frankfort Fair, held each spring, are assuming increased craft importance.

AUSTRIA High standards of craftsmanship are maintained in traditional forms, as well as in the growing body of contemporary work in all media, including wood carving, marquetry, and gilding as well as major works in other craft media. Skilled artisans are employed in the gobelin and glass manufacturing firms in Vienna, one of which designed and made the chandeliers for the new Metropolitan Opera in New York.

Of importance are the international ceramics seminars which have been held annually for the past five years at Gmunden, where selected professional craftsmen have worked and experimented, using the facilities of a porcelain factory, with notable results. These seminars have served as models for similar undertakings in Czechoslovakia and Israel, and there are plans for instituting them elsewhere.

Until recently the Osterreicher Werkbund was the organization for Austrian crafts, but a new movement of the artist-craftsmen has been started, centering around the Austrian Museum for Applied Arts in Vienna.

SWITZERLAND The Swiss Werkbund founded in 1913, organizes exhibits at home and abroad, arranges tours for interested foreigners, maintains a collection of photographs and slides, and organizes a group of experts for counseling on the development of new products. In another field, Heimatwerk, founded in 1930, has helped preserve traditional crafts in small and isolated communities, by providing teachers and retail outlets in the large cities.

Several museums display crafts, notably the Kunstgewerbmuseum in Zurich, and the International Centre of Ancient and Modern Tapestries in Lausanne which holds biennial exhibitions.

The important crafts are ceramics blown and **ITALY** molded glass, smalti for mosaics, furniture and cabinet making, intarsia or inlay, cast and wrought iron, jewelry, enamelling, weaving, decorative fabrics, bookbinding, and gilding. Sophisticated crafts are the work of architects, painters, and sculptors to be found in the major metropolitan areas such as Rome, Florence, Venice, and Milan, where much of the modern architecture and design is centered.

Encouragement is given to the growing body of designer-craftsmen by the many local museums, which hold frequent national and international exhibitions. Notable internationally are the Milan Triennale, the Venice Biennale and the annual exhibition at Faenza. A number of influential periodicals also lend support to art works in all media.

At the root of an inauspicious craft situation lies **FRANCE** the meaning of the word "artisan." Specifically, the artisan is a workman with a job or metier in the smaller industries, so that the plumber or the electrician is on a footing with the silversmith or the glass-blower. Moreover, no worker is eligible for assistance from the Service de l'Artisanat unless he employs at least three apprentices. Thus the craftsman has no real status, either professional or economic, but an important step in the right direction was the recent enactment of a law which designated tapestries as fine arts if not reproduced in a series of more than ten.

The principal crafts are: fabrics, rugs, and carpets; tapestries for which painters design the cartoons, executed chiefly at Aubusson; silk screen and painting on silk, basketry of fine rattan or rustic wicker; wood carving, wood turning, furniture and cabinet making; glass blowing, as at the famous cristalleries of Daum, Baccarat and St. Louis. At Vallauris, in the Maritime Alps, there are many potters, also at Dieulefit in the Drome, at Vence and at Biot where interesting stained glass is made.

The Maison des Metiers d'Art Français in Paris has a permanent display center for French crafts, and has cooperated in producing a directory of craftsmen. The National High School of Decorative Arts in Paris trains designers in the fields of theater, interior decoration, architecture, glass and tapestry. There are many other schools both in Paris and elsewhere.

Craftsmen at the Royal Tapestry Factory still **SPAIN** weave reproductions of paintings by Goya and Velasquez, but at the School for Tapestry in Madrid weavers have used cartoons based on abstract paintings. Murals in tiles, completely contemporary in design, are in production. A number of contemporary craftsmen are associated with the design development organization, Hintrade with headquarters in Madrid.

The traditional crafts in Spain are still practiced by artisans throughout the country. The principal crafts are: carpets, tapestries, and other fabrics; tiles, ceramics; furniture, wood carving, lacquer; gold and silversmithing, wrought iron work; glass, baskets, laces and leather goods.

PORTUGAL Thousands of qualified craftsmen and designers in Portugal remain anonymous, according to tradition; nevertheless, there are certain ceramists and tile makers who have become famous. Designer-craftsmen have been encouraged by the opening of the Interior Gallery in Lisbon which has a permanent exhibition of contemporary tapestries, enamels, jewelry, fabrics, and popular and contemporary ceramics.

AFRICA The indigenous crafts of Africa reflect two disparate cultures, the Mohammedan Arabic civilization in the north along the Mediterranean and the tribal cultures of sub-Sahara Africa. These blend into each other at the borders of the two regions, principally along the coast, where the Mohammedan religion has penetrated into the countries of central Africa.

That the arts and crafts of black Africa have had a great impact on modern culture is now generally recognized. The profound influence of tribal carvings and the bronzes on modern Western art has long been acknowledged. But the first general claim for recognition by the Africans themselves was in the First World Festival of Negro Arts, held under the sponsorship of UNESCO at Dakar, Senegal, in 1966. It is the general opinion, however, that development programs must have national interest and support; a number of the new governments have already established agencies for this purpose.

MOROCCO With Morocco's independence in 1958, renewed impetus sprang up to revive the rich legacy in handcrafts, and to that end, schools were established, including a School of Fine Arts at Tetuan. Cooperatives which plan yearly exhibitions have been developed under the Direction Générale de l'Artisanat at Rabat, which has branches in Fez, Marrakech, Meknes and other towns.

The rich variety of present-day Moroccan crafts includes woven carpets, rugs and tapestries; embroidered materials; pottery, mosaics and tiles; metal work; basketry, and the great variety of leather work, dyed and gilded.

MAURETANIA Moroccan influences are also apparent in the crafts of Mauretania to the south, in jewelry and ornaments, chain-stitch embroidery, musical instruments, wood carving in fine relief, leatherwork—ornamented saddles, boots, bags—and in rugs with colored ornament and sheepskin centers.

ALGERIA Algeria has craft centers at Oran and Algiers. Principal crafts are: weaving, particularly of carpets; jewelry, enamelled silver; wood carving, embroidery and pottery.

TUNISIA Crafts have favorable status in Tunisia today, assisted by the Office National de l'Artisanat. Plans call for regional research and production centers, for sales centers in foreign capitals, and for measures of protection for the craftsmen.

The important crafts of the country include carpets, blanket weaving, brass and copper works, leather goods, jewelry, pottery, tiles, mosaics, glass, and carved architectural stone work.

LIBYA Libya shares the Arabic-Mohammedan tradition with other Mediterranean countries. The Islamic Institute of Arts and Crafts has its headquarters at Tripoli.

U.A.R. In the U.A.R. there is a growing awareness of and education for craftsmenship. The number of contemporary artist-craftsmen is increasing, especially in Cairo. A wide variety of crafts is taught at the College of Applied Arts in Cairo, often with considerable freedom of design. At the American University in Cairo, the ceramics department experi-ments with glazes of desert sands.

In a widely-known experiment a group of child weavers of the village of Harrania, working without cartoons, under the supervision of a Cairo architect, have produced tapestries of notably original design.

The principal indigenous crafts of the country are hand weaving of cotton, silk, wool and linen; tapestry, carpet and rug making; mat making, furniture; ceramics; chased metal work and copper washed with tin; musical instruments; baskets, gazelle skin bags, toys, clay figures, and jewelry of gold, amber, lapis lazuli and turquoise.

SUDAN The Sudan, to the south of the U.A.R., is Mohammedan in culture. There is an art school at Khartoum, its capital.

ETHIOPIA Ethiopia is a Christian country, rooted in early Biblical traditions and culture.

Ethiopian agencies interested in the crafts are the Ministry of Education and Fine Art, Her Majesty's Handicraft School, and the Y.W.C.A., whose classes are also under the sponsorship of Her Majesty.

TANZANIA An effort—led by the Minister of Culture—is being made by the National Arts Council of Tanzania to coordinate all crafts, to raise and maintain standards, to provide materials and tuition, and to arrange exhibitions both at home and abroad.

KENYA UGANDA The crafts of Tanzania, Kenya and Uganda, as well as those of neighboring Rwanda and Burundi, include chiefly mats and basketwork of all kinds, shields and drums of wood and leather; jewelry of metal, cowrie shells and seeds; calabash decoration, and elaborate ornamental beadwork on clothing, fly whisks, and spear handles.

MALAGASY REPUBLIC Formerly Madagascar, this island republic reflects a strong French influence. A partial list of its well-developed crafts includes ceramics, wood carving in large open-work panels; totem pole-like grave markers carved with symbolic figures and deep pile rugs repeating these symbols; applique wall hangings, wood inlay boxes and trays; musical instruments, bamboo work, baskets, and colored straw hats and bags.

NIGERIA Among the wealth of Nigerian crafts are: pottery, textile weaving and dyeing, wood and ivory carving, calabash decoration, raffia weaving and cane works, embroidering and dyeing of leather, glassworks and blacksmithing. Notable are the brass works cast at Benin.

Both the Ministry of Education and the Ministry of Trade are interested in craft development; the Nigerian Arts Council is concerned with higher artistic standards for all the arts. Some crafts are taught at Ahmadu Bello University, at Yaba College of Technology, and at the Abuja and Okigwi Pottery Centers.

GHANA Ghana, the former Gold Coast, is famous for its crafts, especially the Ashanti gold weights, cast by the lost wax process, each a miniature work of art; the chiefs' carved stools; and the traditional Kente cloth, woven in narrow strips, sewn together in patterns of special significance, formerly worn only by chiefs. Other crafts are pottery, leather work, wood and ivory carving, blacksmithing, bead work, gold and silver work, jewelry, broadloom weaving, silk screen printing on paper and cloth, dolls and toys, baskets and mats of bamboo, rattan and reed, and musical instruments.

Crafts have usually been carried on as a family or village activity. An effort is now being made to revive interest in them as part of the country's social and economic development. Interested in the crafts are the Ministries of Art and Culture, of Community Development, and of Social Welfare; also the Ghana Institute of Art and Culture. Crafts, especially ceramics are taught in art schools in several cities.

LIBERIA The culture and crafts of Liberia are similar to those of Ghana and Sierra Leone, neighboring countries with related tribes. Their crafts include weaving of Kente cloth and embroidering on clothing. Hand printing, either batik or tie-dyed, is done on imported white cloth in traditional short lengths. Woodwork takes the form of ceremonial masks, tables and stools, and relief carvings done for wall panels and doorways. Ceramics are mostly country pots, often of quite large size, used for storing water and for cooking. Jewelry consists of gold and silver bracelets and rings in traditional designs. Basketry of palm and bamboo is decorative as well as utilitarian.

In the government-sponsored Kindeja Cultural Center in Monrovia each of the tribes has a hut where craftsmen work and sell their products. In another experiment, conducted at Numba, under joint Swedish, American and Liberian sponsorship, a recreation center provides handcraft instruction of high quality for the three thousand inhabitants of this mining town. Both the Department of Education and the Department of Information and Culture are concerned with crafts, and there are several school where they may be studied. A Liberian Arts and Crafts Association was recently organized.

SIERRA LEONE The Ministries of Education, Trade and Industry, Tourism and Social Welfare are all interested in the crafts, and there is a Sierra Leone Arts and Crafts Society.

UPPER VOLTA Since the Upper Volta is primarily agricultural, the crafts there are a domestic and seasonal activity, practiced during the dry season from December to April.

Blacksmiths and potters are closed castes, ranking high socially. Leather craftsmen, of more open caste, also are numerous. Nouna is a center for smiths, masons and builders who also make furniture, tools and weapons. Metalsmiths also work in copper, silver, aluminum and gold. Craft organizations are nonexistent.

MALI The outstanding crafts are metal work, weaving, and wood carving; important products are drums, leather bags and saddle bags, and ebony figures and chests with metal adornment. The National Institute of Mali Arts at Bamake exhibits and sells crafts.

SENEGAL All of the countries along the west coast of Africa show much European influence. This is perhaps epitomized in Senegal whose capital, Dakar, is a beautiful French colonial city, and whose sophistication in the arts was shown by its taking the lead in calling the First World Festival of Negro Arts in 1966, under the leadership of its president, the poet Dr. Leopold Sendar Senghor.

Crafts are under the Directeur de l'Office Senegalais de l'Artisanat.

○ NORTH AMERICA The indigenous work of the Indians and Eskimos, in both the United States and Canada, is being revived under government sponsorship. A notable school in Santa Fe, New Mexico, has drawn Indian students from all over the United States to study and create work based on their old traditions. In Canada the work with the Eskimos has produced worldwide recognition of their carvings and prints, and the Indians of Canada are hoping for similar encouragement.

U.S.A. In the United States there is but one national organization, the American Craftsmen's Council,

and to it is due much of the credit for the present stature of the crafts in this country. Tax-exempt as an educational institution but without government subsidy, it is supported solely by contributions and membership fees. It maintains the Museum of Contemporary Crafts and publishes the magazine Craft Horizons, which has international coverage of the crafts. The Council holds national and regional conferences, and maintains a file of craftsmen's work with photographs and slides which is increasingly used by architects, decorators and others wishing to commission craft works. It also maintains a library and research service and rents color slides for lectures or for study. Since 1964 it has given office space and personnel help to the World Crafts Council, a UNESCO organization with representatives in fifty-four countries, which was formed in 1964 through its invitation and cooperation.

The Smithsonian Institution in Washington, D.C. has already performed a notable function in respect to the crafts through its circulation of traveling exhibitions.

The American craft scene is becoming increasingly internationalized, through craftsman participation in many government programs such as the Fulbright Fellowships, the Peace Corps, and the A.I.D., and in the privately endowed fellowships administered by the International Institute of Education, and in the programs of UNESCO and the International Labor Organization, but in general there has been no government program of assistance, as is true for all the arts of the U.S.A.

A revival of interest in crafts has been fostered CANADA by several provincial governments which carry on active promotional programs. Among the Eskimos of the Far North, a government program encouraging soapstone sculpture goes back some twenty years.

The Canadian Handicraft Guild operating from Montreal has branches and retail outlets, where only the work of Canadian craftsmen is sold. It has an extensive collection of both traditional and modern Canadian crafts; biennial exhibitions are held of work from all over the country. The Canadian Craftsmen's Association operates from Ottawa. The Canadian government has had under consideration the establishment of a national research and experiment center for the visual arts, which would include the fine crafts.

Great impetus was given the craft movement by the centennial year celebrations, notably by Expo '67, in which crafts were shown in important national pavilions. An exhibition of Canadian contemporary crafts was assembled for the government of Canada building, and this collection has been bought as the nucleus of a permanent craft collection for the museum at Prince Edward Island, the first in Canada to begin showing crafts on the same basis as painting and sculpture. Also during the centennial year a traveling exhibition of Canadian "fine crafts" was selected by the National Gallery of Canada.

The aborigines, who peopled Australia before AUSTRALIA ○ the coming of the Europeans, were a nomadic people who decorated their weapons, tools and bodies with beautiful stylized designs; their bark paintings are finding a ready market. Today craftsmen are beginning to study their work and also that done in neighboring Pacific islands, especially New Guinea.

Pottery is the main craft and the Potters Society of New South Wales has been an important factor in the developing interest in crafts. At the Sturt Association of Mittagong, pottery, weaving and woodwork are produced by full-time craftsmen. The principal contemporary crafts are ceramics, sculpture, jewelry, weaving, fabric printing, wood carving and furniture; and one or more of these crafts are taught at the six art schools in cities throughout the country.

NEW ZEALAND There is an increasing interest among the Maori people in their own culture, and a realization that the peculiarly Maori skills—carving and taniko weaving—must be rescued while there is still time. The Rotorua Maori Arts and Crafts Institute has recently been started by the Government to preserve Maori traditions. A very few Maoris are experimenting with the materials used by European craftsmen.

Because of the economic problems of New Zealand, which call for stringent import restrictions, New Zealand craftsmen find great difficulty in obtaining the necessary materials and tools. As in Australia, the most important crafts are ceramics and weaving; New Zealand wool is excellent.

○ LATIN AMERICA In Mexico, Guatemala, and the countries of Andean South America, European conquerors found a rich native culture with highly developed gold working and textile techniques which have persisted in the folk arts. In time the European, chiefly Spanish, technical and artistic influence spread over Latin America, with some Asiatic and African elements later brought in by trade or slavery.

Today crafts have lost much of their vitality. The problems were discussed at the Seminar on Latin American Arts and Crafts held at Mexico City in October 1965 under the sponsorship of the Government of Mexico and UNESCO, with participation by representatives of most of the Latin American countries.

Contemporary Latin American artist-craftsmen are slowly opening new roads. There is a desire on the part of the individuals among them to experiment and turn out creative works. There are very few schools that teach this approach, and so far there are only a few outstanding individual craftsmen. Many artists still go abroad to study, and the immigration of European craftsmen is having a vitalizing effect.

VENEZUELA In Venezuela a group of serious artist-craftsmen is developing, centered around the Museum of Fine Arts at Caracas. By contrast, the indigenous arts of Venezuela are relatively sparse, with some ceramics, basketry and jute rug making in the villages.

The principal crafts are ceramics, glass-blowing, enamelling, silver and goldsmithing. A strong influence has been the world-famous architecture of the University of Venezuela at Caracas, which incorporates craft works in a wide variety of media, designed by some of the foremost European artists.

GUYANA The Ministry of Education is now providing that all pupils in secondary schools have three years of craft training. Plans are under way to develop the cottage industries.

BRAZIL Influenced by the important work of the country's architects, Brazilian contemporary crafts have a solid basis in contemporary design. They are, however, influenced by the craft attitudes of Europe, where Brazil's most important artists have studied, and where tapestries, mosaics and stained glass are designed by painters and executed by artisans. Indigenous crafts are primitive, and although they are now being collected and preserved, have little effect on contemporary work.

In the north around Recife and Bahia the folk art influence is strongest, and many artists, including several well-known tapestry designers, work in this area. Rio de Janeiro is still a main center of activities with its Museum of Modern Art, which, however, seldom shows crafts. Sao Paulo, in the south, is especially notable because its important international biennial art exhibition at the Museum of Modern Art is gradually being opened to those crafts which qualify as arts.

URUGUAY The modern craft movement is beginning to gain importance in Uruguay. The first students to graduate from the University of Applied Arts are now establishing themselves, each in his own craft, and the inauguration of an international biennial exhibition of applied arts at Punte del Este has been an important step forward. Also of considerable interest is some of the work of artist-craftsmen collaborating with architects.

PARAGUAY A partial list of traditional Paraguayan crafts includes Fianduti lace, cloth made at Yatayty village, gold puzzle rings, guitars, ceramic figures made at Asuncion, and decorated gourds for mate.

ARGENTINA The students of folklore art are working continually to save the craft traditions, in symposia, schools and institutes. Indigenous crafts exist in all the media, especially textiles, leather, basketry, primitive pottery, wood carving.

In the field of contemporary design, there are many artist-decorators, graduates of the National School of Fine Arts and the National School of Ceramics, who are working in various media. An important group is the Center for Ceramic Arts and a group of tapestry designers is developing. These modern crafts are carried on almost entirely in Buenos Aires, and many potters, painters and sculptors teach in their studios in that city.

CHILE In Chile not only is there increasing interest in the crafts on the part of the public, but in Santiago, the capital, there is a group of artist-craftsmen who work seriously in a contemporary manner. The principal craft media are taught in the School of Applied Arts in Santiago, a branch of the School of Fine Arts. Also of interest is a school of stonecutters in Santiago for sculptors and craftsmen, with special provisions for architects experimenting in designs for their own work.

Some indigenous work is still done throughout the country, especially in two villages in which the whole population works in ceramics. In the Folk Art Museum in Santiago one may see examples of native crafts.

BOLIVIA In Bolivia today, in spite of rich traditions, the crafts make very little contribution to the national economy, although the Ministry of Education and Culture and a few private and semi-official organizations are making efforts to develop them. A very few Bolivian craftsmen have traveled and exhibited abroad.

PERU Until its conquest by the Spanish, Peru was the capital of the far-flung Inca empire and the center of a flourishing culture. Today the principal indigenous crafts are weaving, ceramics, silver and gold work, leather tooling, wood carving and basketry, many of these in the same rich variety as the pre-Columbian artifacts to be seen in the Lima museums and private collections. These crafts are mostly carried on by artisan-craftsmen, who continue to use traditional designs, chiefly in the highland centers and on the north coast. An effort has been made to establish various governmental aid programs.

In Peru, the concept of the artist-craftsman has not been developed. Recently, however, a National Association of Peruvian Craftsmen was formed. Organizations concerned with the crafts include the Miraflores Art Center in Lima, and the Handicraft Center, also in Miraflores, maintained by the Division of Technical Education of the Ministry of Public Education, which also conducts training schools for adults in twenty-eight areas. Lima is the center of an international development program for crafts for the Andean countries.

ECUADOR In Ecuador, the folk arts are still rich and varied. Of particular distinction are the rugs and hangings made of native wool by native craftsmen using old techniques, under the direction of a Hungarian artist, long a resident of Ecuador.

COLOMBIA Although rich in ancient handcrafts, Colombia is only now beginning to develop modern craftsmanship under a very few leaders, some of whom are connected with the University of the Andes in Bogota. A few artist-craftsmen have experimented with contemporary design and some have achieved international status.

PANAMA Notable in Panama is the finely worked appliqué in bright colored cottons done by the San Blas Indians. There is a National Service for Craft and Small Industries, in Chiltre, Herrera.

GUATEMALA In this country more than a million pure-blooded Mayans live much as did their ancestors, weaving and wearing almost the same costumes, traveling much the same mountainous roads to buy and sell at distant markets.

Weaving is the most important craft, still often done on belt looms in laid-in patterns characteristic of special areas; also ikat weaving is done. Cotton is used in the warm lowlands and wool in the mountain areas. The pottery is glazed and unglazed, including a burnished, pre-conquest type, often fired in a hole in the ground. There are also baskets, mats and bags made of string and rope. Wood carving is an ancient Mayan art, often combined with painted decoration in chests or masks. There are carved gourds. Lanterns and candlesticks are made from tin.

A number of government agencies are concerned with the crafts, but as yet there is no overall organization concerned with their development. The Universidad Popular in Guatemala City teaches woodwork and ceramics, and a few painters and sculptors work in craft media.

MEXICO Mexican crafts had their origin in the remarkable Mayan and Aztec cultures which flourished in Mexico before the arrival of the Europeans. The Conquistadores brought Spanish crafts and design. From the combination of these two currents came Mexican folk arts, which are among the most flourishing in the world today. Craftsmen have had wise and articulate leadership, and Mexico ranks with India in government support of folk crafts. Leadership in all aspects of the folk art development has been provided by the National Museum of Popular Arts, with its program of research, technical and economic assistance, competitions, and exhibitions, with special emphasis on the maintenance of standards. Government financing through designated banks is an important feature of the craft scene.

Under the Ministry of Public Education, craft schools and workshops are maintained in all regions of the country. There are several schools of higher grade in Mexico City, among which the School of Design and Craftsmanship of the Institute of Fine Arts is especially devoted to the developing of contemporary craftsmanship. There is a National Association of Craftsmen and a large number of artist-craftsmen have united to establish the Bazar Sabado.

Oaxaca is a craft center rich in fabrics and embroideries, ceramics, lacquered gourds, ornamental tinware and tooled leather, baskets and raffia bags. In nearby Mitla are noteworthy rebozos and scarves; near too, is the village where a famous woman potter makes her burnished black ceramic ware shaped as animals, birds and mermaids. Other area specialties are the revived silver industry of Taxco, and the ceramic work of Tonala, characteristically in bird forms.

WEST INDIES Recently, with the development of new political and economic ties, and with a new market opened for many by the burgeoning tourist trade, the various islands are starting revivals of their arts and crafts, each in its own way.

TRINIDAD TOBAGO In Trinidad and Tobago government workshops teach straw weaving and embroidery, and the Art Society at Port of Spain has classes in pottery, enamelling and metal work. Local family workshops produce pottery and filigree jewelry, some in traditional East Indian patterns.

JAMAICA In Jamaica, the Craft Development Agency has been working for some time with the aid of experts from the International Labor Office of the United Nations on a reorganization of the handcraft industries in straw work, wood, ceramics, and textiles.

CUBA Embroidery, pottery from Calabazar, basketry, and other crafts are being revived by the Bureau of Applied Arts of the National Council of Culture. and by the Ministry of Education, whose program provides instruction in special arts and crafts schools and also for amateur groups.

PLATE 1. CERAMIC FACE POT, COIL BUILT IN SARA-
GUM, SEPIK REGION

PLATE 2. COTTON BATIK PANEL BY TOICHI MOTONO, KYOTO

PLATE 3.   CERAMIC SLAB CONSTRUCTION, 28 X 24 IN.
(71 X 61 CM.), BY HIROAKI MORINO, KYOTO

PLATE 4. "WALK," CERAMIC CONSTRUC-
TION BY KAZUO YAGI, KYOTO

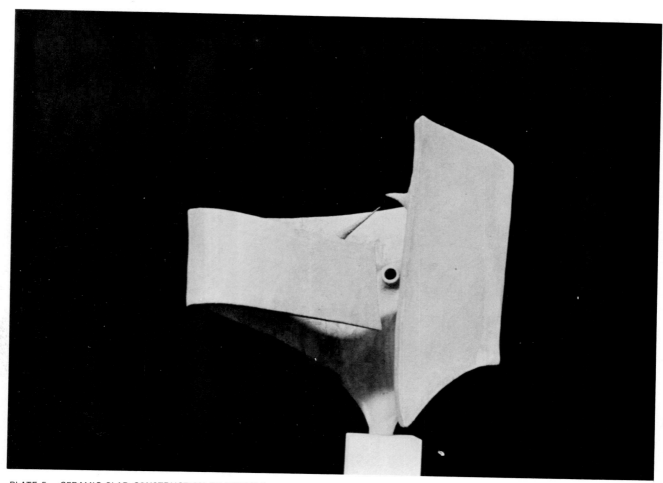

PLATE 5. CERAMIC SLAB CONSTRUCTION BY TADASHI
KAWAI, KYOTO

PLATE 6. CERAMIC JAR BY TOYO KANE-
SHIGE, BIZEN PREFECTURE

PLATE 7. CERAMIC BOWL BY YU FUJIWARA, BIZEN
PREFECTURE

PLATE 8. CERAMIC DISH
BY SHOJI HAMADA, TOCHIGI
PREFECTURE

PLATE 9. KOREAN WOOD PADDLES FOR SHAPING THE POT. PATTERNED SURFACE PERMITS BETTER GRIP ON CLAY

PLATE 10   BASE IS BEATEN WITH ROUGH STICK. INDENTATION ON SURFACE ALLOWS BETTER HEAT ABSORPTION

PLATE 11.   BUILDING POT WITH COILS

PLATE 12.   SHAPING THE POT

PLATE 13. CHARCOAL BRAZIER IS LOWERED INTO POT TO DRY INSIDE, THUS HELPING TO RETAIN THE GROWING SHAPE

PLATE 14.   THE BRAZIER CAN BE RAISED AND LOWERED

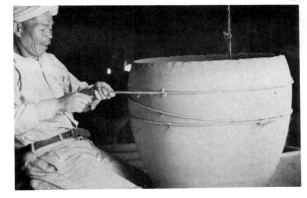

PLATE 15. A ROPE IS BOUND AROUND THE WIDEST POINT TO KEEP THE POT FROM SAGGING UNDER THE WEIGHT OF ADDED CLAY

PLATE 16.   BUILDING WITH MORE COILS

PLATE 17.   COMPLETING THE POT

PLATE 18.   THE FINISHED POT OF RED CLAY IS CARRIED OUTSIDE TO DRY, THEN FINISHED BY TYING A ROPE TO IT AND FLOATING IT IN A VAT OF MANGANESE AND LEAD GLAZE. A LITTLE IS ALLOWED TO ENTER THE POT SO THAT AS IT IS ROTATED, IT IS GLAZED BOTH INSIDE AND OUT. IT IS FIRED AT A LOW TEMPERATURE

PLATE 19. "YUKIGUNI," DETAIL OF KOGIN EMBROIDERY, COTTON THREAD ON
COTTON, OVERALL 31 X 23 IN. (80 X 60 CM.), MADE IN THE WORKSHOP OF MISAO
KIMURA, SENDAI

PLATE 20. "BRIGHTNESS," WOVEN TAPESTRY, 11½ X 13
FT. (3.2 X 4.0 M.), BY HIROZO MURATA, KYOTO

PLATE 21. "THE VIOLENT WAVE," BAM-
BOO FLOWER CONTAINER BY SHOUNSAI
SHONO, OITA PREFECTURE

PLATE 22. CHILD'S MASK, PAPIER-MACHE

PLATE 23. KITES, PAPER ON BAM-
BOO BY STUDENTS OF ISAMU
KENMOCHI, TOKYO

PLATE 24. COOKING POT, CAST BRASS

PLATE 25. LACQUERED WOOD SCREEN, 25 IN. HIGH (64 CM.), BY KIM BUYNG KI, SEOUL

PLATE 26. DETAIL OF *KASURI* KIMONO, WARP DYED
IN HAEBARU

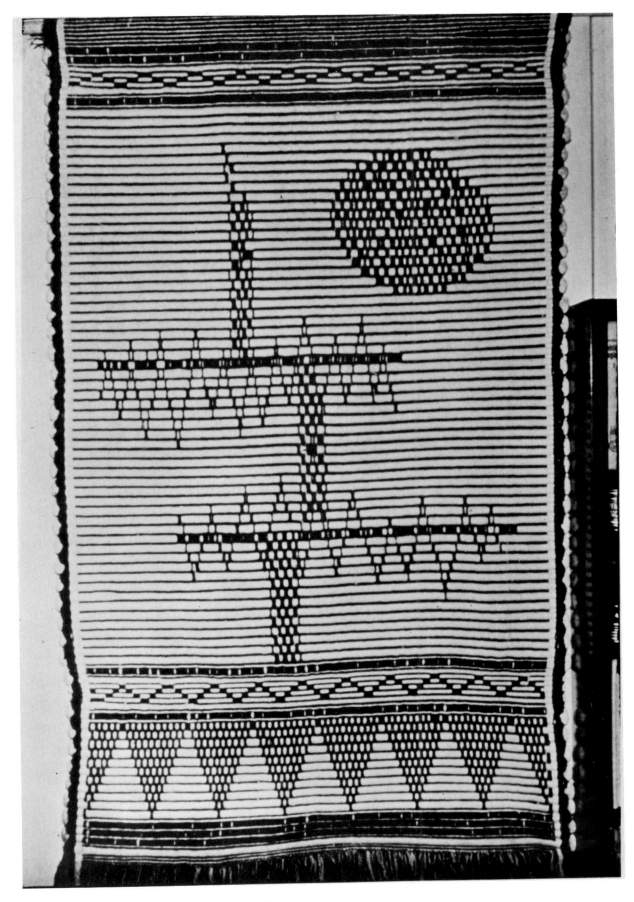

PLATE 27. "MOON AT THE WINDOW," WALL HANGING
BY ILSE VON RANDOW, AUCKLAND

PLATE 28. STONEWARE POT BY HELEN
MASON, WELLINGTON

AUSTRALIA

PLATE 29. STONEWARE BOTTLES,
THROWN AND CUT, 25, 24 AND 18 IN.
HIGH (64, 61 AND 46 CM.), BY COLIN
LEVY, NEW SOUTH WALES

PLATE 30. THROWN AND SLAB STONEWARE POT, 23 IN. HIGH (59 CM.), BY MILTON MOON, BRISBANE

PLATE 31. "MALAY-WOMAN," BATIK BY TAY MO-LEONG, PENANG

BATIK MAKING IN DJOKJAKARTA, JAVA

PLATE 32.   A BATIK WORKER PUTS WAX INTO A SMALL IRON POT OVER A CHARCOAL BURNER

PLATE 34.   BATIK IS DIPPED INTO A TUB OF BROWN DYE MADE FROM THE BARK OF THE SAGO TREE

PLATE 35.   *SRUNI* DESIGN REQUIRES SIX MONTHS TO COMPLETE

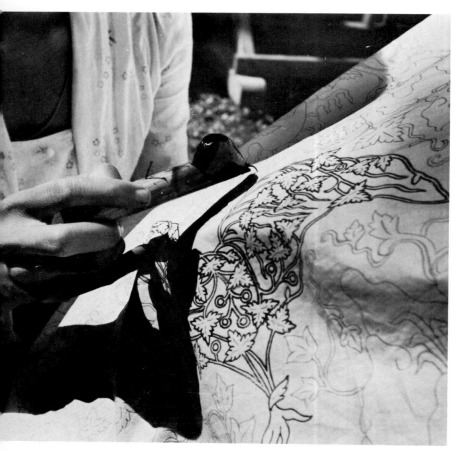

PLATE 33.   WOMAN USING THE *TJANTING* — SMALL COPPER CONTAINER WITH LONG SLENDER SPOUT FOR PAINTING THE DESIGN WITH HOT WAX

PLATE 36.   IN THE BATIK MARKET OF DJOKJAKARTA

48

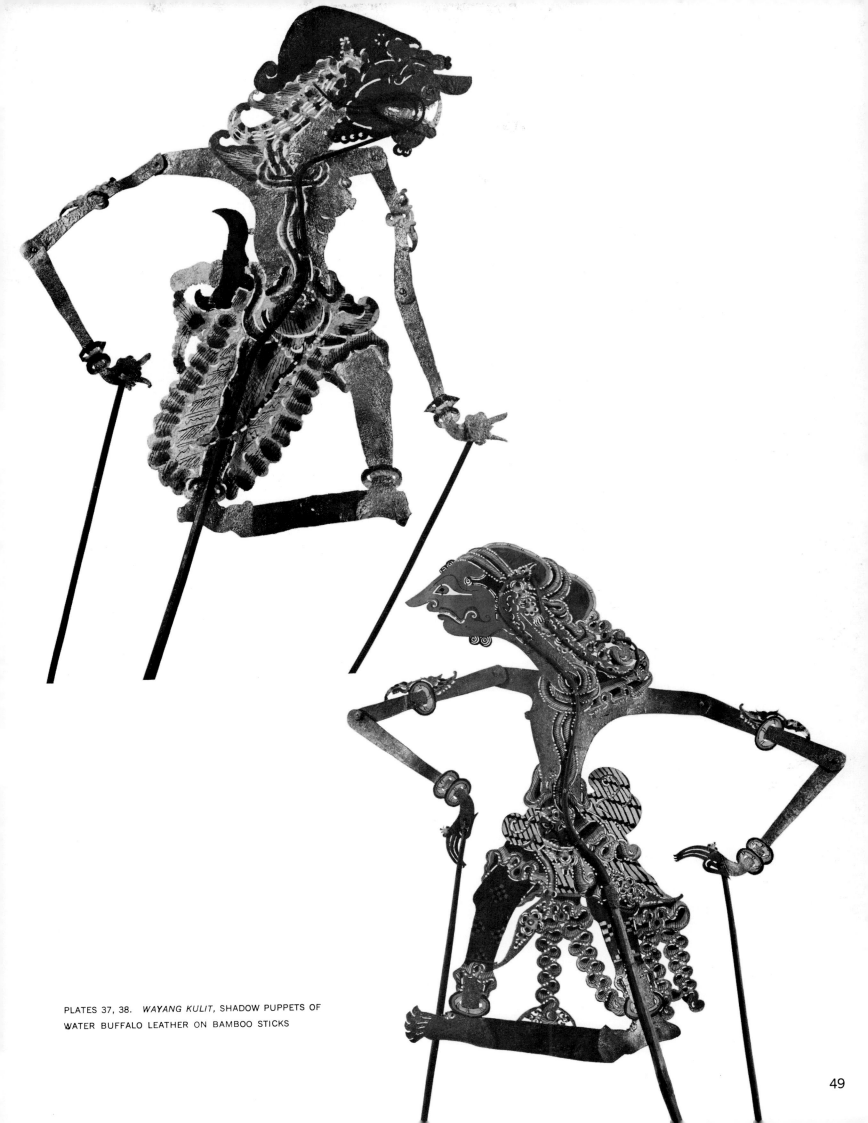

PLATES 37, 38. *WAYANG KULIT*, SHADOW PUPPETS OF
WATER BUFFALO LEATHER ON BAMBOO STICKS

49

THAILAND

(FACING) PLATES 41 TO 46. CALICO PRINTING IN SANGANER NEAR JAIPUR. THE CLOTH IS DIPPED AND WRUNG OUT IN A SOLUTION OF TANNIC ACID. WITH THE BLACK PASTE IN THE DISH, THE BACKGROUND IS PRINTED WITH A FELT-COVERED WOOD BLOCK ON THE FACE OF WHICH THE REPEATING DESIGN UNIT HAS BEEN CARVED. THE CLOTH IS THEN BLOCKED WITH A TAN PASTE CONTAINING ALUM. BLOCKED IN THEIR RESPECTIVE BLACK AND TAN PASTES, THE CLOTHS ARE BEATEN ON THE WASH STONES OF THE SANGANER RIVER. THEY ARE THEN STIRRED FOR FIVE OR SIX HOURS IN A HOT SOLUTION OF ALIZARIN WHICH, COMBINING MORDANTICALLY WITH THE ALUM PASTE, DEVELOPS THE RED. DIPPED IN A COW DUNG AND WATER SOLUTION AND STORED OVERNIGHT IN THE CRAFTSMEN'S HOUSES, THE LENGTHS OF CLOTH ARE FINALLY WASHED AND SPREAD OUT ON THE RIVER BANK WHERE THEY ARE KEPT DAMP FOR THREE DAYS UNTIL THE COLORS ARE DEEP AND RICH

PLATE 39. WOVEN SILK PLAID

PLATE 40. BROCADE, SILK WITH METALLIC THREAD

PLATE 48. SILVER ANKLETS FROM BEZWADA, ANDHRA

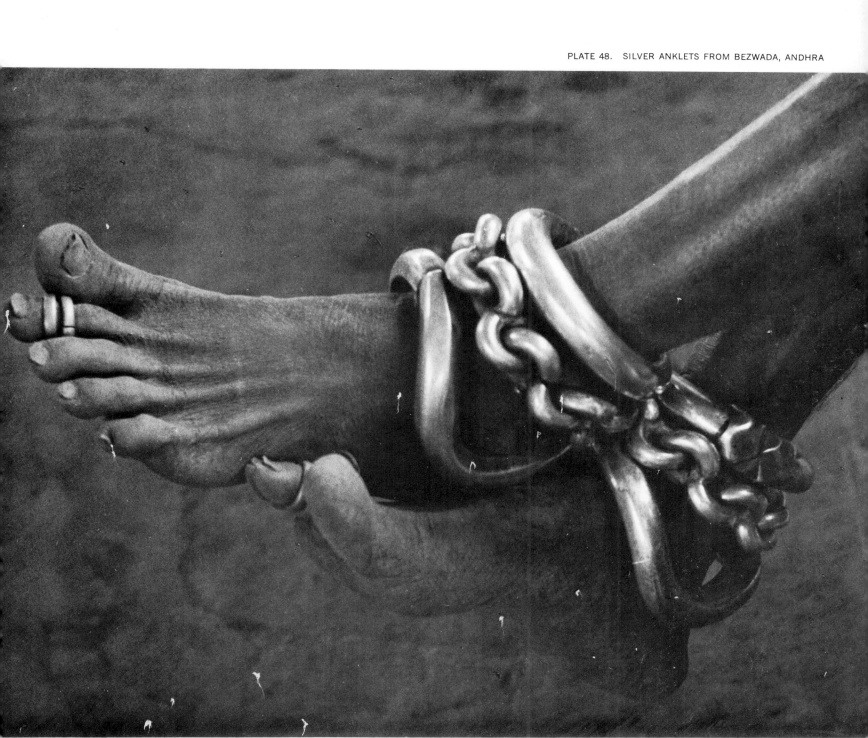

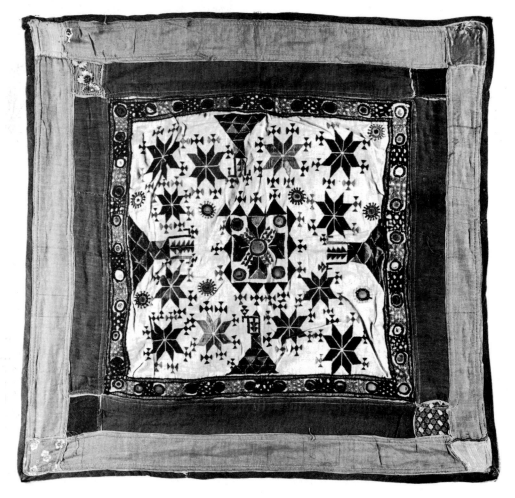

PLATE 49. EMBROIDERED PANEL WITH MICA INSETS FROM GUJRAT

PLATE 50. COTTON APPLIQUE PANEL FROM GUJRAT

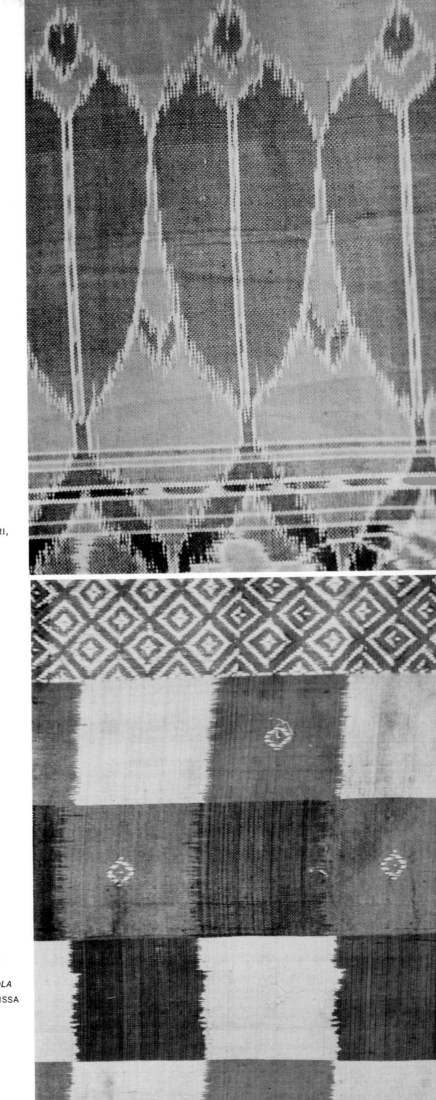

PLATE 51. DETAIL OF COTTON SARI,
PATOLA (WARP DYED), FROM ORISSA

PLATE 52. DETAIL OF SILK SARI, *PATOLA*
TECHNIQUE AND BROCADE, FROM ORISSA

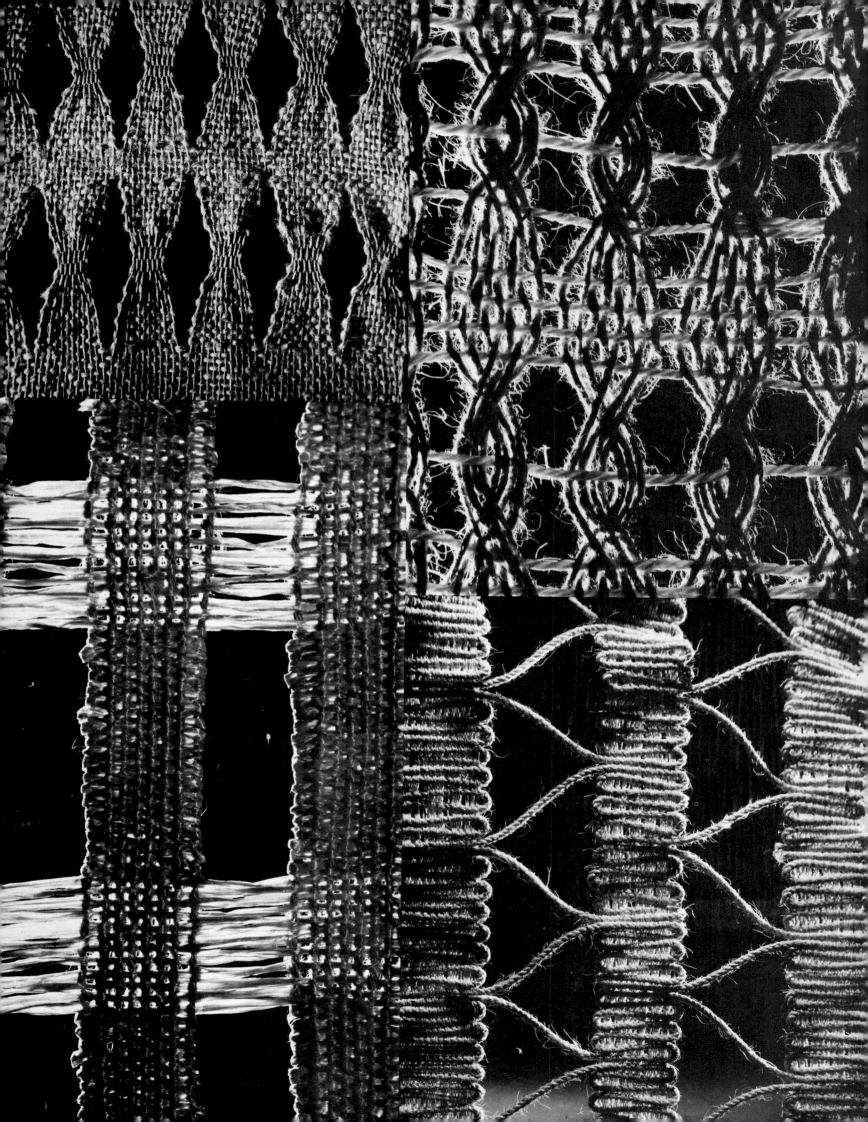

PLATE 57. WALL HANGINGS IN EXHIBITION AT BOMBAY WEAVERS' SERVICE
CENTER OF THE ALL INDIA HANDLOOM BOARD

PLATE 58. HORSE, CARRIED IN RELIGIOUS PROCESSIONS; PAPER ON BAMBOO FRAME, 57 IN. HIGH (145 CM.), FROM BENGAL

PLATE 59. DOLL WITH SARI, MICA EYES AND MOUTH, FROM GUJRAT

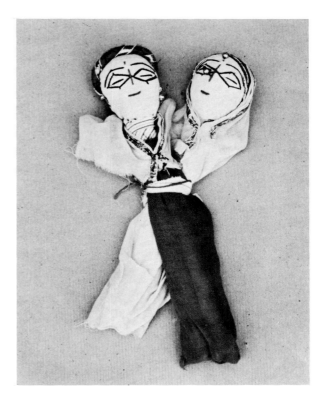

PLATE 60. CONJUGAL DOLLS FROM GUJRAT

PLATE 61. FANTASY-ANIMAL TOY FROM NATIONAL DESIGN INSTITUTE, AHMADABAD

PLATE 62. LIDDED BASKET OF SIKHI GRASS, 20 X 14 IN. (51 X 37 CM.), FROM BIHAR

PLATE 63. CARVED WOOD UTENSILS AT BAZAAR IN BANGALORE, MYSORE

PLATE 64. STREET POTTER IN THE POLIANTHOPE DISTRICT OF MADRAS

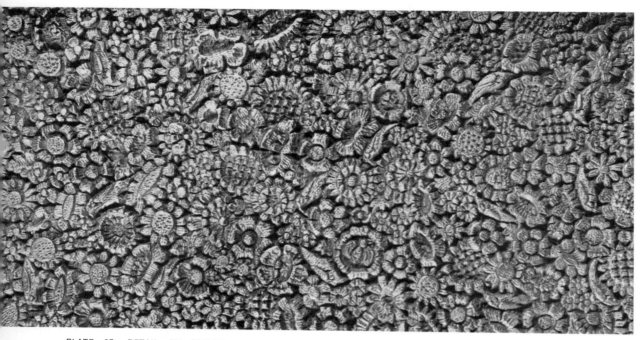

PLATE 65. DETAIL OF CARVED
WOOD PANEL FROM KASHMIR

PLATE 66. DETAIL OF CREWEL
EMBROIDERY, WOOL ON COTTON,
FROM KASHMIR

PLATE 67. DETAIL OF WOVEN WOOL SHAWL, WITH
TRADITIONAL *BUTA* MOTIF, FROM KASHMIR

CEYLON

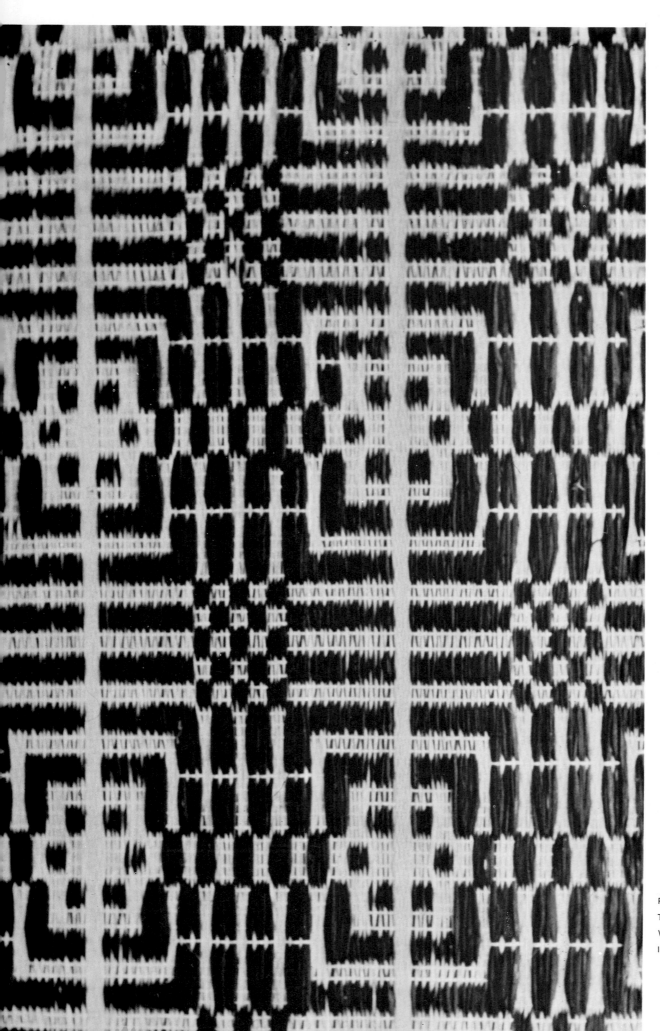

PLATE 68. DETAIL OF SLEEPING MAT, TOTAL SIZE 36 x 70 IN. (92 X 177 CM.), WOVEN OF FIBER FROM THE *HANA* PLANT IN THE DUMBARA VALLEY

PLATE 69. BOY WORKING ON A DUMBARA SLEEPING MAT. WITH THIS FLOOR LOOM THE WEAVER SITS ON THE ALREADY WOVEN MATERIAL ROLLING IT BEHIND HIM AS THE WORK PROGRESSES. THE TRIPOD OF STICKS WHICH HOLDS CLUSTERS OF COLORED FIBER IS MOVED ALONG AHEAD OF HIM

PLATE 70. THE VILLAGE POTTER OF KELANIYA TRAINS HIS SON

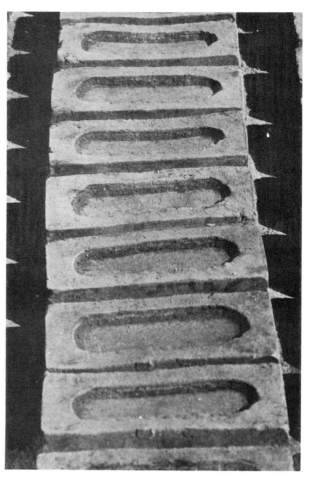

PLATE 71. THIS SINGLE WOOD MOLD MAKES HUN-
DREDS OF HAND-PRESSED BRICKS IN KATMANDU

PLATES 72, 73. HAND-PRESSED BRICKS ARE STACKED
AND FIRED IN KILN MADE OF THESE BRICKS

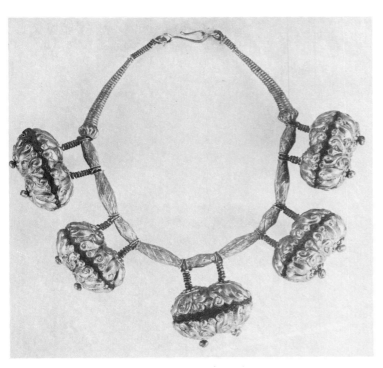

PLATE 74. NECKLACE, BEATEN BRASS JOINED BY
PITCH WITH TALLOW, FROM KATMANDU

PLATE 75. PAPIER-MACHE FESTIVAL FIGURE IN KATMANDU

PLATE 76. WOMEN IN THE STREET STRINGING THE
LONG WARP FOR A SARI, KATMANDU

PLATE 77. DETAIL OF SAND-CAST MURAL, MOTIFS FROM MOHENJO-DARO SEAL AND SWAT FOLK ART, BY SALAH-UD-DIN, LAHORE

PLATE 78. SPINNER OF COTTON IN LAHORE

PLATE 79. FELTED TENT RUG BY THE NOMADS OF
NORTHERN IRAN

PLATE 80. EMBROIDERED SHEEPSKIN JACKET FROM
NORTHERN IRAN

PLATE 81.   VILLAGE POTTER'S WORKSHOP NEAR BEIRUT.

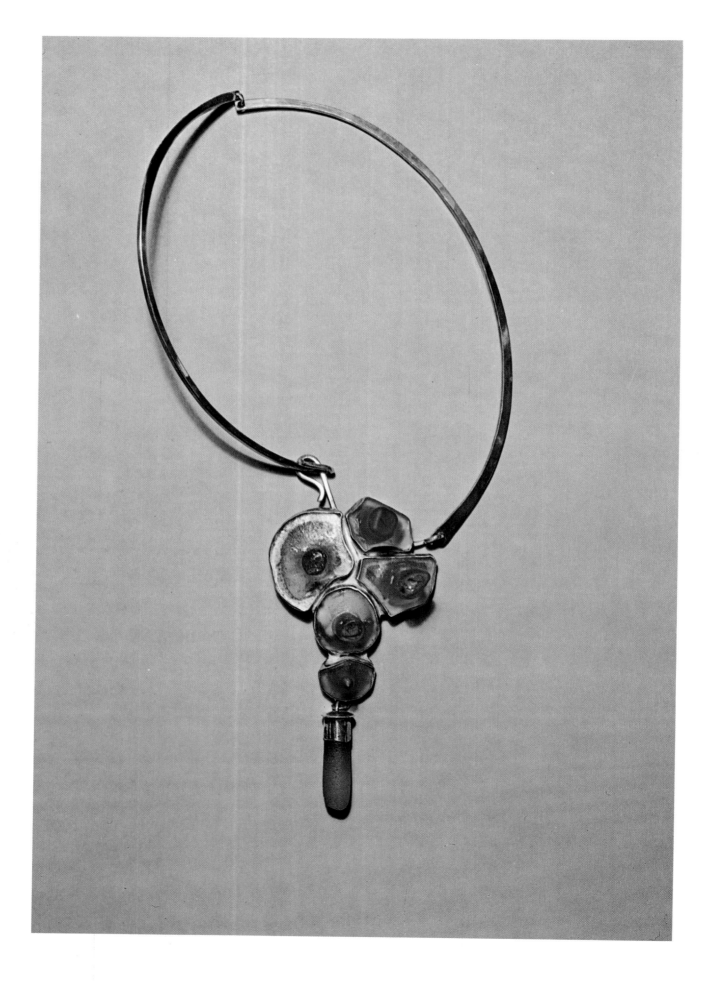

PLATE 82. NECKLACE, SILVER SET WITH ANCIENT GLASS FRAGMENTS FROM
ROMAN SITES ON LAKE CESAREA, BY FINI LEITERSDORF, TEL AVIV, EXECUTED AT
MASKIT ISRAELI ARTS AND CRAFTS CENTER

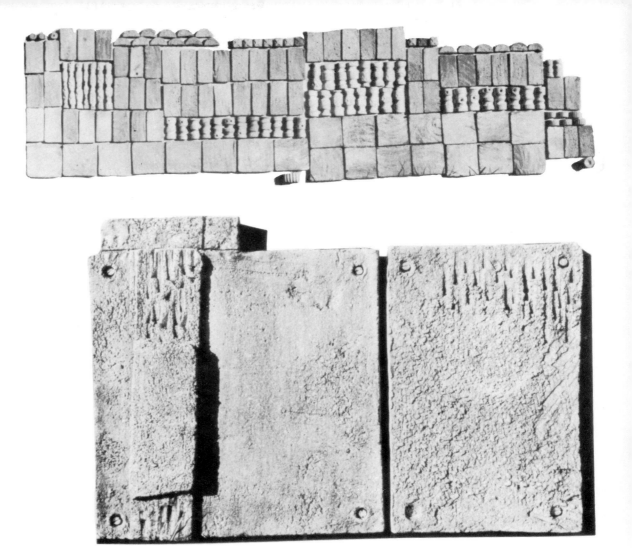

ARCHITECTURAL CERAMIC TILES
BY (PLATE 83) GDULA OGEN,
(PLATE 84) JEAN MAYER, AND
(PLATE 85) HANNAH CHARAG-
ZUNTZ

71

PLATES 86, 87. SUN-BAKED
POTS IN BAGHDAD

PLATES 88, 89. HAND-BLOCKED
COTTON SCARVES FROM ISTANBUL

PLATE 90. MURAL FOR ANKARA BUILDING, INCISED
GLAZED TILES, EACH 12 X 12 IN. (30 X 30 CM.), OVER-
ALL 7½ X 10 FT. (2.25 X 3 M.), BY JALE YILMABASAR,
ISTANBUL

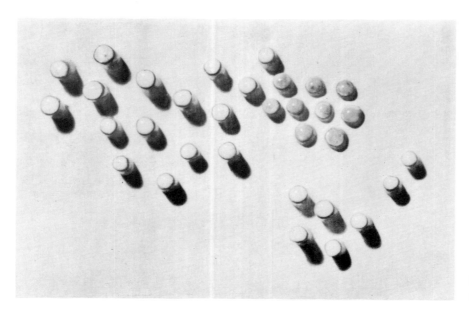

PLATE 91.   CERAMIC PANEL, 12 X 8 IN.
(31 X 20 CM.), BY FUREYA, ISTANBUL

PLATE 92. WOVEN CUSHION COVER FROM THE ANOXIA
AREA OF CRETE

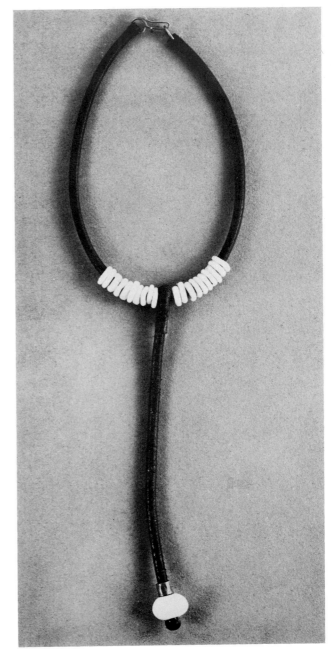

PLATE 93. NECKLACE, LEATHER AND
GLASS BEADS BY THE LATE ISMINI
MANOUSAKI, CRETE

PLATE 94. WELDED STEEL BAR AND BOTTLES, 5 FT.
HIGH (1.52 M.), BY PHILOLAOS, ATHENS

PLATE 95. "COMPOSITION IN WHITE AND BLACK," TAPESTRY, 7 X 18 FT. (2.10 X 4.60 M.), BY BALEV DIMITAR

PLATE 96. "POLYTIQUE," TAPESTRY, 8 X 18 FT. (5.5 X 2.5 M.), BY JAGODA BUIC, ZAGREB

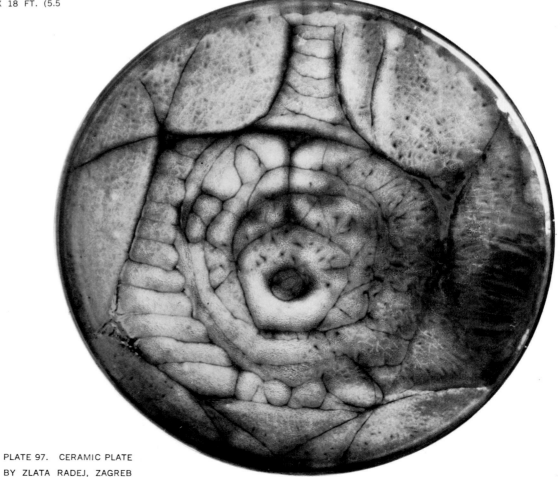

PLATE 97. CERAMIC PLATE BY ZLATA RADEJ, ZAGREB

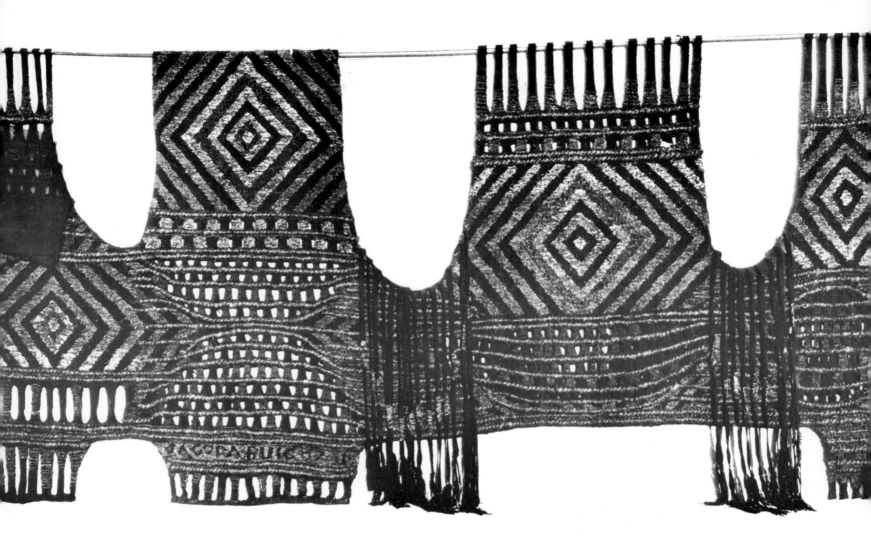

PLATE 98.   "RELIEF METER," MOVABLE ALUM-
INUM ELEMENTS, 39 X 39 X 7 IN. (100 X 100 X
18 CM.), BY VJENCESLAV RICHTER, BELGRADE

HUNGARY

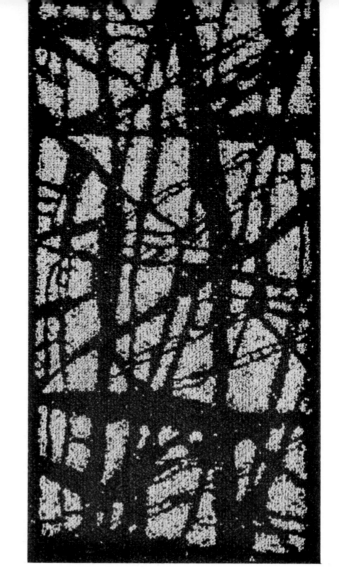

PLATE 99.   BOUCLE RUG, 27 X 55 IN. (70 X 140 CM.),
BY KLARA CSAGOLY, FOLDVAR

RUMANIA

PLATE 100.   CERAMIC CONSTRUCTION BY PATRICIOU
MATTEESCU, BUCHAREST

PLATE 102. NESTING
WOOD DOLLS

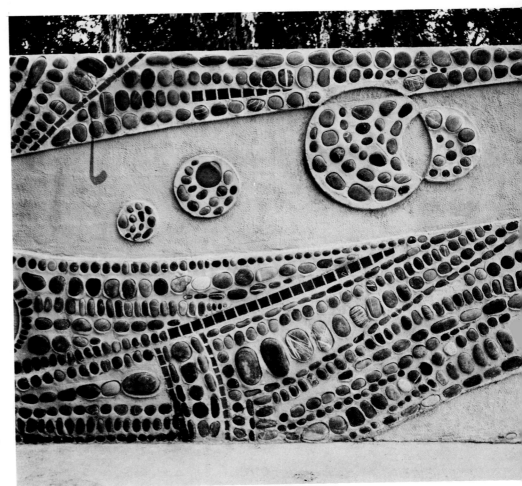

PLATE 101. CEMENT WALL INLAID WITH
STONES AND GLASS IN TOWN OF SOCHI
DESIGNED AND EXECUTED BY EVGENY
ALBIN AND IVAN DROBYSHEV, MOSCOW

PLATE 103. *"LA NUIT BLANCHE,"* WOOL WALL HANGING,
9 X 6½ FT. (3 X 2 M.), BY WOJCIECH SADLEY, WARSAW

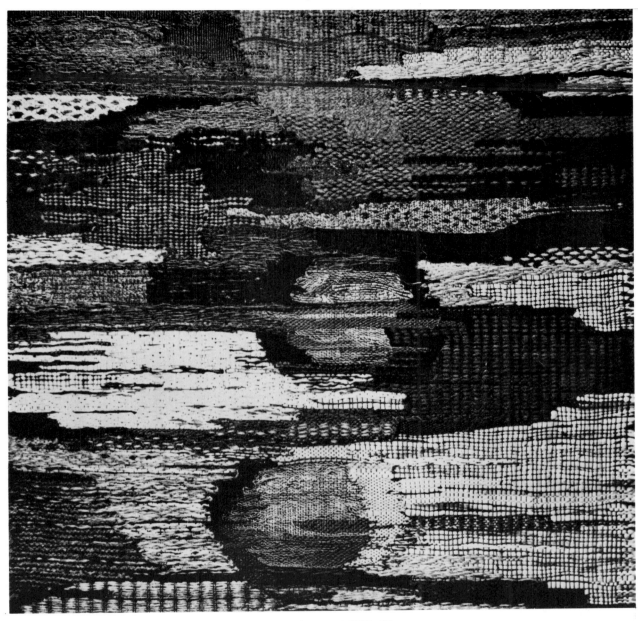

PLATE 104. "MIRAGE," TAPESTRY, 49 X 60 IN. (125 X 155 CM.), DESIGNED BY
WANDA TELAKOWSKA; EXECUTED BY DANUTA SZARRAS EYMONT, WARSAW

PLATE 105. TRADITIONAL *WYCINAKI* (PAPER CUTOUT)
OF BIRDS AND HERBS, 8 IN. DIAM. (20 CM.)

PLATE 107. GLASS BOTTLE, BLOWN AND PRUNTED, 18 X 9 IN. (47 X 24 CM.), BY RENE ROUBICEK FOR BOR GLASSWORKS AT NOVY BOR

PLATE 106. BLOWN GLASS COLUMN BY P. GRUSS AND P. HLAVA, PRAGUE

PLATE 108. BLOWN GLASS VASE, 7½ X 8 IN. (19 X 20 CM.), BY VLADIMIR JELINEK FOR KAROLINKA GLASS-WORKS, MORAVIA

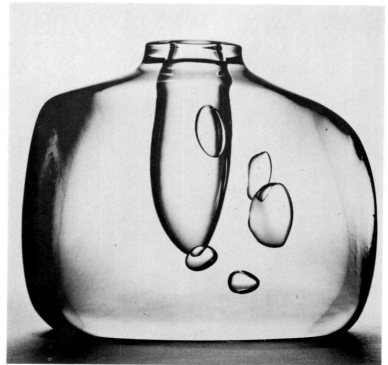

PLATE 109. PORCELAIN CONSTRUCTION
BY LUBOR TEHNIK

PLATE 110. "DAWN FOR AESOP," LACE
PANEL, 42 X 78 IN. (108 X 198 CM.), BY
LUBA KREJCI, PRAGUE

PLATE 111. "CERAMIC FACTORY," CERAMIC CONSTRUCTION BY KAREL NEPRAS, PRAGUE

PLATE 112.   SECTION OF THE GLASS WALL IN THE HALL OF THE INTERNATIONAL
RAILWAY UNION, PARIS, BY STANISLAV LIBENSKY AND JAROSLAVA BYCHTOVA,
EXECUTED BY ZELEZNY BROD GLASSWORKS

PLATE 113.   STONEWARE POT, 7½ X 12 IN. (19 X 30.5 CM.), BY KYLLIKKI SALMENHAARA, HELSINKI

PLATE 114.   BLOWN AND MOLDED GLASS
FORMS BY TIMO SARPANEVA, HELSINKI

PLATE 115.   BLOWN GLASS GOBLETS BY
NANNI STILL, HELSINKI

PLATE 116.   BLOWN AND BLISTERED
GLASS FORM BY KAJ FRANCK, HELSINKI,
FOR WAERTSILA AT NOTSJO

PLATE 117. LAMINATED WOOD FORM BY
TAPIO WIRKKALA, HELSINKI

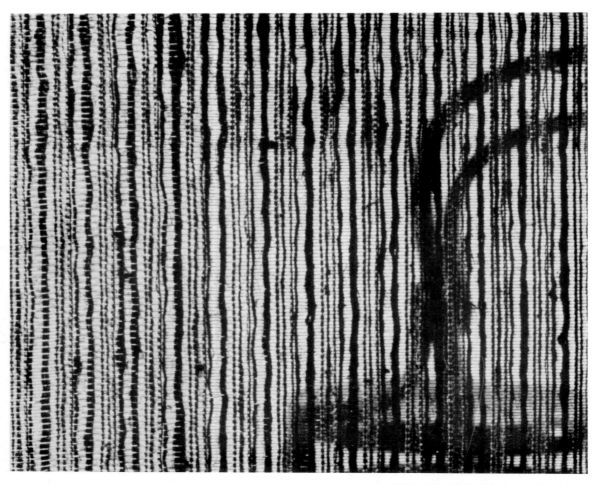

PLATE 118. "DRAGONFLY," WOVEN LINEN WITH COP-
PER THREAD BY MARJATTA METSOVAARA, HELSINKI

90

PLATE 119. SCREENED COTTON PRINT BY VUOKKO
ESKOLIN, HELSINKI

PLATE 120. "MEDUSA," SCREENED COTTON PRINT BY
MAIJA ISOLA FOR MARIMEKKO, HELSINKI

PLATE 121. THROWN CERAMIC VASE, 13 IN. DIAM. (34 CM.), BY RAIJA TUUMI, HELSINKI, FOR WAERTSILA, ARABIA

PLATE 122. GLASS BRICKS WITH HOOKS BY OIVA TOIKKA, HELSINKI

PLATE 123. HANGING BY OILI MAKI, LEPPAVAARA

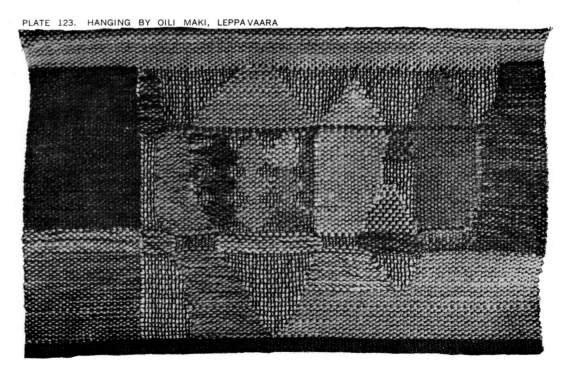

PLATE 125. SILVER CANISTERS BY BIRGER HAGLUND, STOCKHOLM

PLATE 124. SILVER FLASKS BY SIGURD PERSSON, STOCKHOLM

PLATE 126. CHASED GOLD BOWL BY CLAES GIERTTA, STOCKHOLM

PLATE 127. STONEWARE SPHERES BY KARIN BJOR-
QUIST, STOCKHOLM, FOR GUSTAVSBERGS FABRIKER

PLATE 128. DRINKING GLASSES BY ERIK HOGLUND,
MALMO, FOR AFORS GLASBRUK

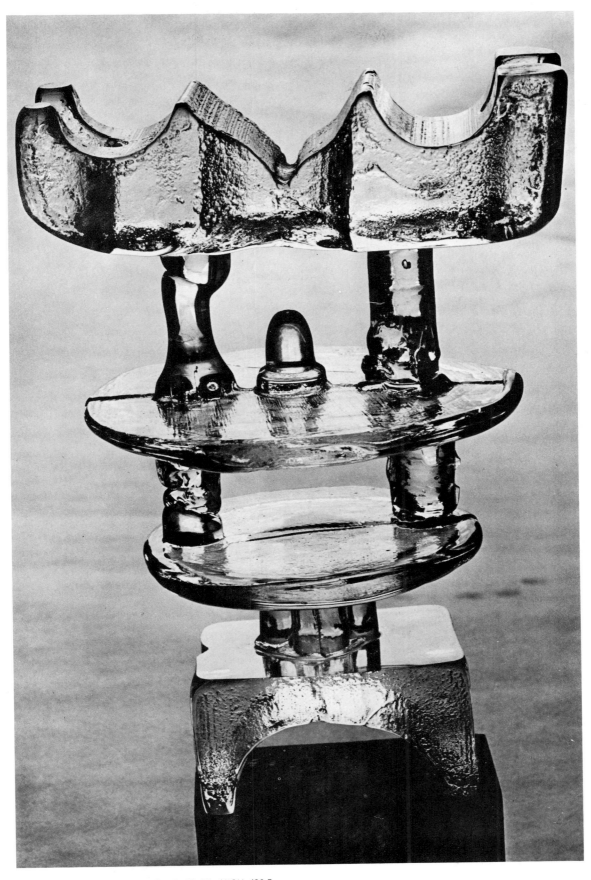

PLATE 129. "TOWER," SANDCAST, 12 IN. HIGH (30.5 CM.), BY BERTIL VALLIEN, MALMO, FOR AFORS GLAS-BRUK

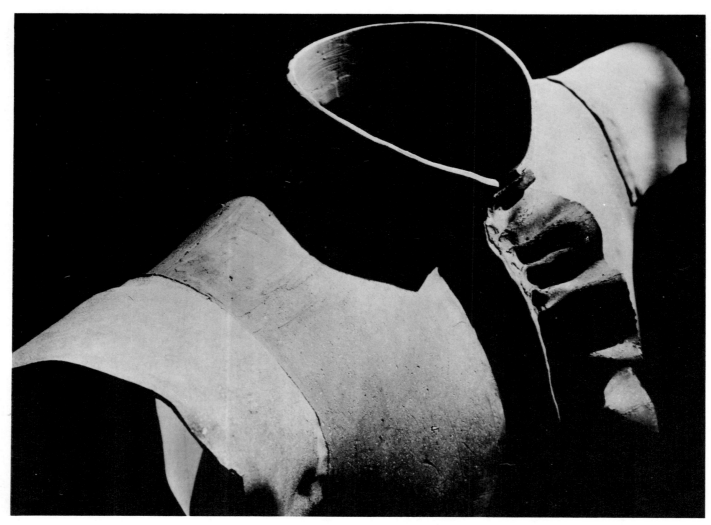

PLATE 130. "BLOUSE," UNGLAZED EARTHENWARE, 24
IN. HIGH (61 CM.), BY HERTHA HILLFON, STOCKHOLM

PLATE 131. CERAMIC WALL IN PUB DEPARTMENT STORE
BY BENGT BERGLUND, STOCKHOLM, EXECUTED AT
GUSTAVSBERGS FABRIKER

PLATE 132. "HAPPY NEW YEAR," CHANGEABLE APPLI-
QUE WITH ZIPPERS, VELVET, SILK AND COTTON, 6½ X 4½
FT. (2 X 1.4 M.), BY MARGARETA HALLEK, STOCKHOLM

PLATE 133. COAT OF WOVEN WOOL AND LEATHER BY
BIRGIT ULLHAMMAR, STOCKHOLM

PLATE 134. VASES, SILVER AND ENAMEL, BY GRETE
PRYTZ KORSMO, OSLO, FOR TOSTRUP

PLATE 136. GLASS BOTTLES BY AKSEL MORCH, OSLO,
FOR NORSK GLASSVERK

(FACING) PLATE 137. DETAIL OF A DOUBLEWEAVE
WOOL COAT BY KRISTI SKINTVIET, FREDRIKSTAD, FOR
PLUS CO-OP

PLATE 135. STONEWARE JAR BY ERIK PLOEN, OSLO

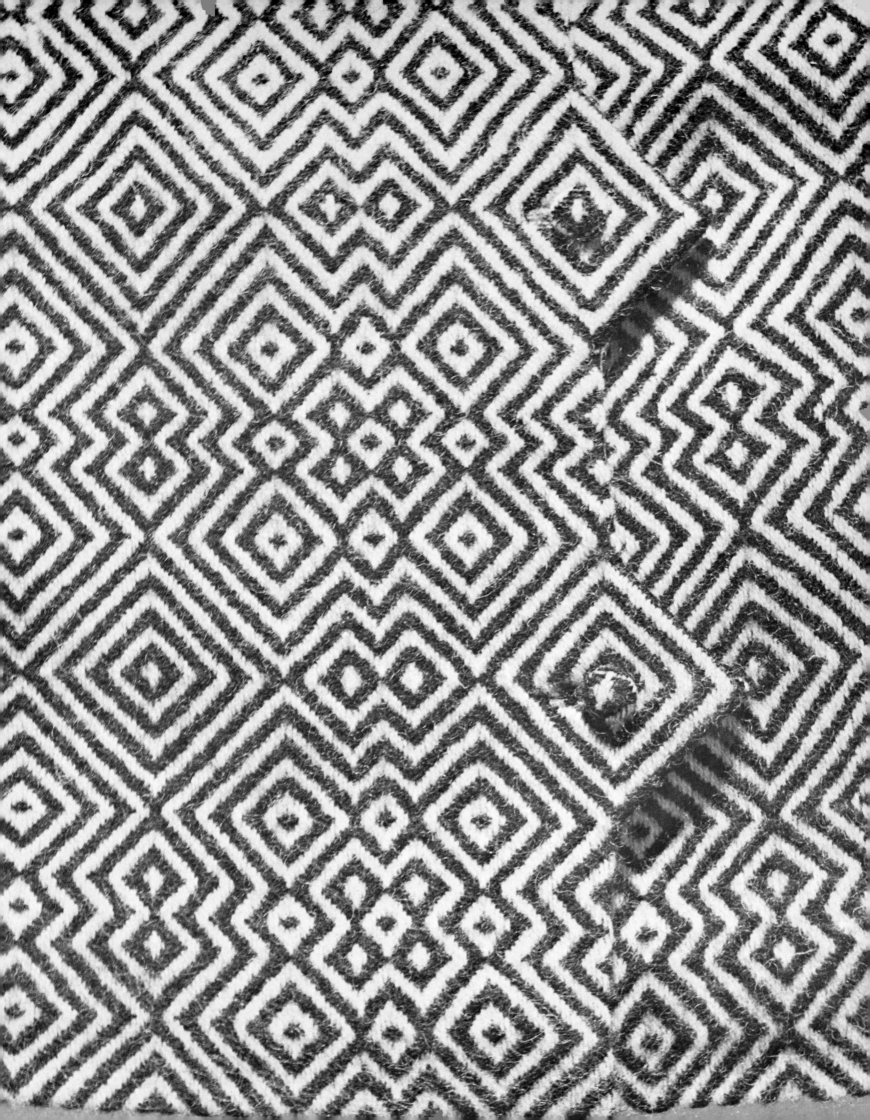

DENMARK

PLATE 138. TEAK CHAIR BY HANS WEGNER, COPEN-
HAGEN, FOR JOHANNES HANSENS MOBELSNEDKERI

PLATE 139. STONEWARE FOUNTAIN BY CHRISTIAN
POULSEN, KONGENS LYNGBY

PLATE 140. STONEWARE PITCHER BY HERMAN KAHLER, MAESTVED

PLATE 141. URETHANE FOAM CHAIR, 30 X 46 X 39 IN. (76 X 117 X 99 CM.), BY GUNNAR AAGAARD ANDERSEN, DRONNINGMOLLE

PLATE 142. STONEWARE RELIEF BY ERIK MAGNUSSEN, FOR BING AND GRONDALL, COPENHAGEN

PLATE 143. "FIGURES," CERAMIC, 21½ IN. (55 CM.), BY BIRTE WEGGERBY, CHARLOTTENLUND

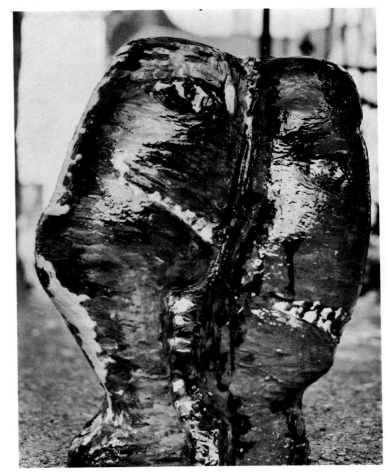

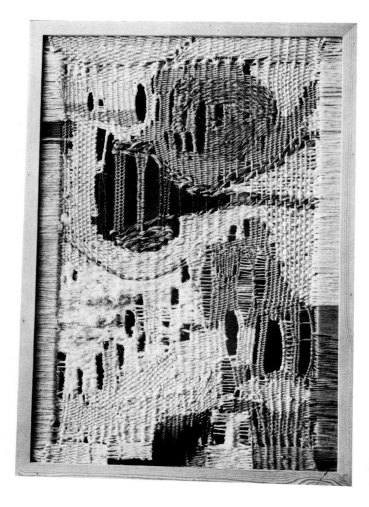

PLATE 144. "DAWN," WOVEN PANEL, 32 X 22 IN. (82 X 55 CM.), BY GRETE BALLE, COPENHAGEN

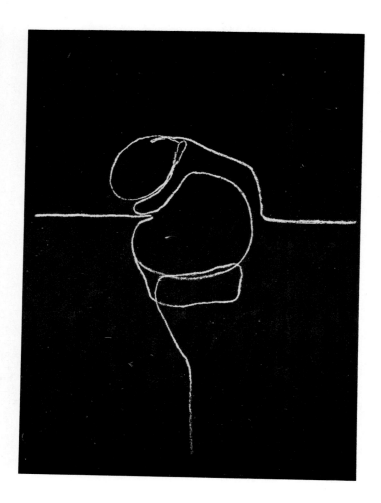

PLATE 145. "SIGN," TAPESTRY, 10 X 7 FT. (3 X 2.2 M.), BY JAN GROTH, NYKOBING

PLATE 147. "THE HONEYMOON," TAPESTRY, 6½ X 1½
FT. (2 X .5 M.), BY MARY DAMBIERMONT, BRUSSELS

PLATE 146. "ENJOYING THE CAR," CERAMIC, 26 IN.
HIGH (66 CM.), BY PIERRE CAILLE, BRUSSELS

PLATE 148. CERAMIC PLAQUE BY LOUISE SERVAES, ANTWERP

PLATE 149. "VASE D'OR," EMBROIDERED APPLIQUE, BY CORINE TOUSSEIN, BRUGES

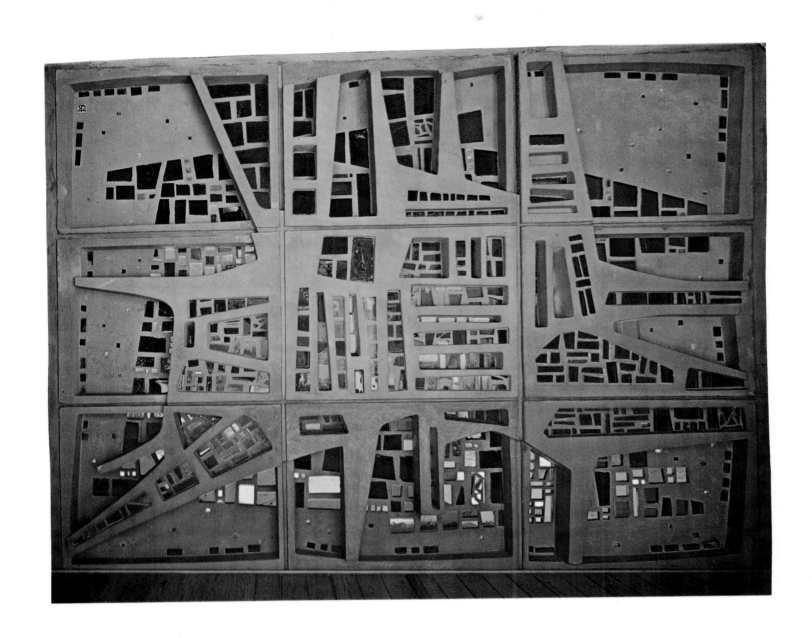

PLATE 150.   STAINED GLASS AND CONCRETE WALL, 8 X
10 FT. (2.4 X 3 M.), IN PRIVATE RESIDENCE, BY GEORGE
STAES, BEVEREN-WAAS

PLATE 151. TAPESTRY BY CHRISTIANE SCHULZ,
TOULOUSE

PLATE 152. STONEWARE VASE BY
FRANCINE DEL PIERRE, PARIS

PLATE 153. STACKED KILN OF THE *CENTRE NATIONAL
DES ATELIERS EDUCATIFS* AT CLAIREAU, CHEVREUSE

PLATE 154. "LOCK," WOOL TAPESTRY, 6¾ X 5 FT.
(2.05 X 1.50 M.), BY PABLO PICASSO; EXECUTED BY
ALGERIAN CRAFTSMEN

PLATE 155. BOOKBINDING, PARCHMENT AND BLACK
BOX CALF IN SLIGHT RELIEF, BY CLAUDE STAHLY,
PARIS, FOR *L'ORDRE GREC* BY FRANCOIS CALI, PUB-
LISHED BY ARTHAUD

PLATE 156.   CERAMIC FORM BY NINO CARUSO, ROME

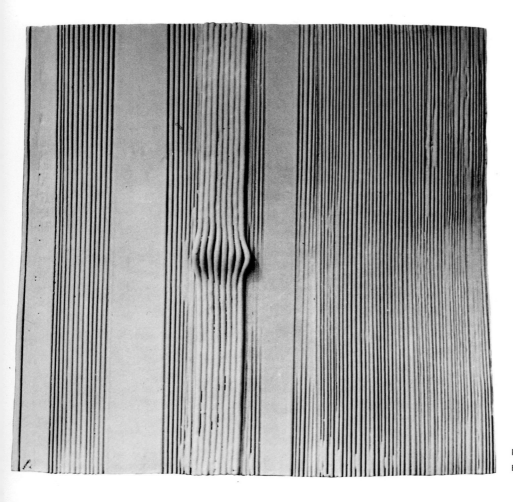

PLATE 157.   CERAMIC TILE, 24 X 24 IN. (60 X 60 CM.),
BY LUCIETTI, VICENZA

PLATE 158.   STONEWARE FLASK, 20 IN. HIGH (51 CM.),
BY GUIDO GAMBONE, FLORENCE

PLATE 159. "PALINURO," HAND KNOTTED WOOL RUG
BY RENATA BONFANTI, BASSANO DEL GRAPPA

PLATE 160. "ANTIQUE LOVERS," STONEWARE, 5 FT.
LONG (1.6 M.), BY LEONCILLO, ROME

PLATE 161. BOWL, ENAMEL ON COPPER, BY PAOLO DE
POLI, PADUA

PLATE 162. CAST SILVER CANDELABRA, 12 IN. HIGH
(30.5 CM.), BY FRANCO CANNILLA, ROME

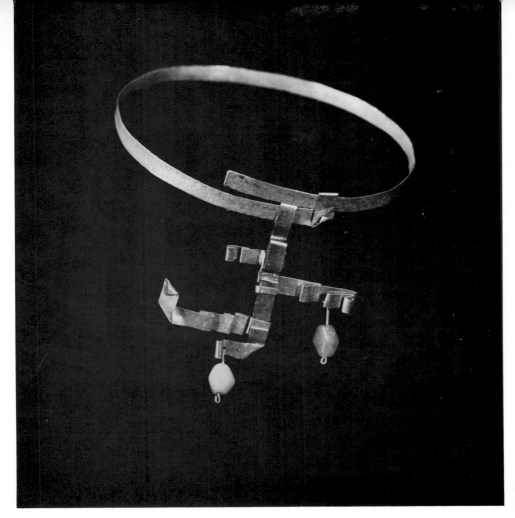

PLATE 163. NECKLACE, SILVER WITH TURQUOISE, BY
MIRELLA FORLIVESI, FLORENCE

PLATE 164. BRACELET, YELLOW GOLD WITH ENAMEL,
TOPAZ AND SAPPHIRES, BY GIO POMODORO, MILAN

(FACING) PLATE 167. DETAILS OF BASKETS AND WOOL RUG, CAGLIARI, SARDINIA

PLATE 165. FORM OF CRYSTAL AND GOLD LEAF, 17 IN. HIGH (43 CM.), BY LUCIANO GASPARI FOR SALVIATI AND CO., MURANO, VENICE

PLATE 166. VASE, 14 IN. HIGH (35 CM.), BY ARCHI-MEDE SEGUSO, MURANO, VENICE

PLATE 168. CRYSTAL CHANDELIER FOR THE AUSTRIAN EMBASSY, LONDON BY HANS HARALD RATH, FOR J. AND L. LOBMEYR, VIENNA

PLATE 169. DETAIL OF CRYSTAL CHANDELIER FOR THE NEW THEATER, LUXEMBOURG, BY HANS HARALD RATH, FOR J. AND L. LOBMEYR, VIENNA

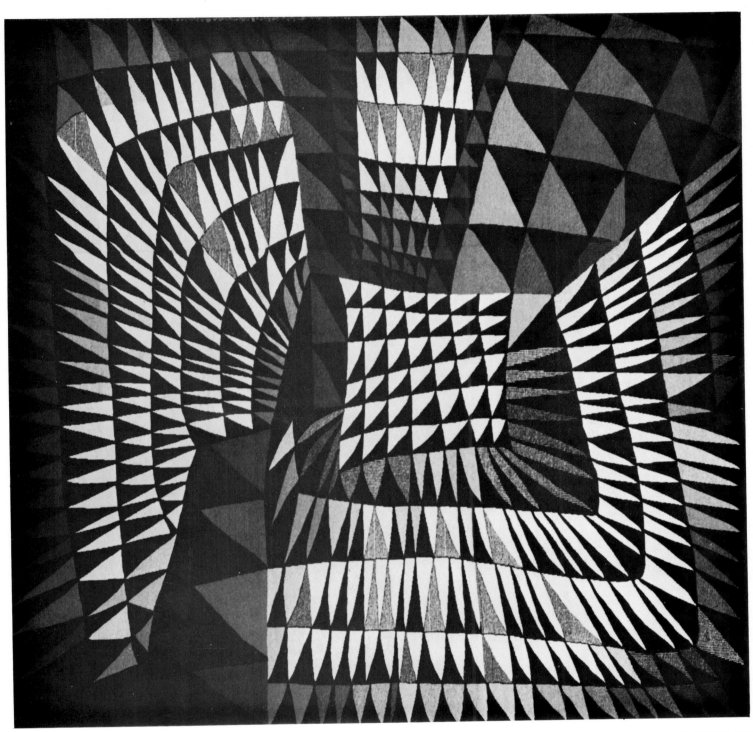

PLATE 170. *"MODULATION CENTRALE,"* TAPESTRY, 122 X 122 IN. (310 X 310 CM.), BY MARIA PLACHKY, VIENNA

PLATE 171. PENDANT, GOLD WITH PEARL INSET, BY
SEPP SCHMOLZER, KLAGENFURT

PLATE 172. CERAMIC FORM BY KURT OHNSORG,
GMUNDEN

118

PLATE 173. WOVEN PANEL BY ERNA SCHILLIG, LUCERNE

PLATE 174.   SECTION OF A WOVEN CONSTRUCTION
165 X 13 X 13 IN. (418 X 33 X 33 CM.), BY ELSI GIAUGUE

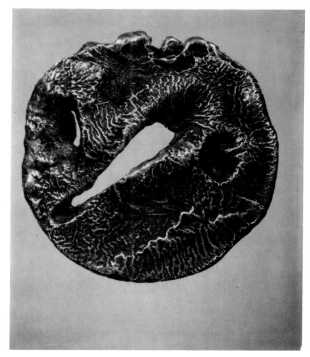

PLATE 175.   GOLD PIN BY LANGENBACHER AND WANK-
MILLER, LUCERNE

PLATE 176.   PIN, GOLD WITH NIELLO, BY
HANS RUDI WAGNER, VAUFFELIN

PLATE 177.   BRACELET, GOLD WITH QUARTZ, BY RITA
HUBBARD, ROMANSHORN

PLATE 178. MURAL, MOSAIC OF NATURAL STONES IN
RESIDENCE, BY ROSE MARIE EGGMANN, GENEVA

PLATE 179. WOOL TAPESTRY, 49 X 53 IN. (124 X 135
CM.), BY LILLY KELLER, MONTET

PLATE 180. "THE KNOT," TAPESTRY OF WOVEN BANDS,
INTERLACED AND DRAWN UP TO FORM LOOPS, 10 X
6½ FT. (3 X 2 M.), BY HERMAN SCHOLTEN, BAAMBRUGGE

PLATE 181. CUT CRYSTAL STRUCTURE
BY WILLEM HEESEN, LEERDAM

PLATE 182. "MOVING GHOST," GOLD PIN WITH GAR-
NET CRYSTALS, BY ANNEKE SCHAT, AMSTERDAM

PLATE 183. HAMMERED AND POLISHED ALUMINUM
SHOULDER-PIECE BY GIJS BAKKER, SOESTDYK

PLATE 184.   DOWNDRAFT KILN WITH THE LARGEST
VASE, 57 IN. HIGH (145.8 CM.), THROWN BY MEINDERT
ZAALBERG, AT THE ZAALBERG POTTERY, OMMEN

PLATE 185.   CERAMIC POT THROWN IN THREE PARTS,
16 IN. HIGH (41 CM.), BY ADRIEK WESTENENK,
AMSTERDAM

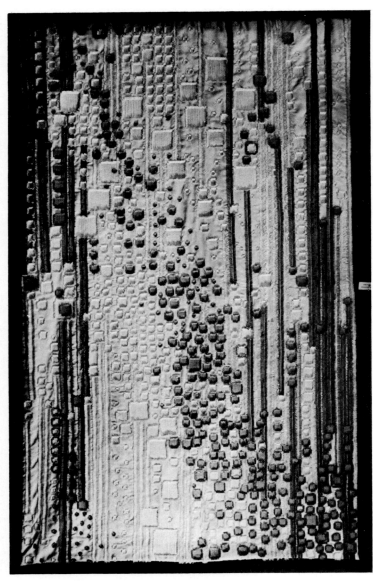

PLATE 186. EMBROIDERED APPLIQUE BY LOTTE
HOFMANN, UBERGAILDORF

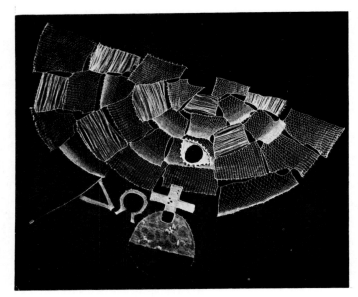

PLATE 187. LACE CHURCH VESTMENT BY
HANNENUTE KAMMERER, MUNSTER

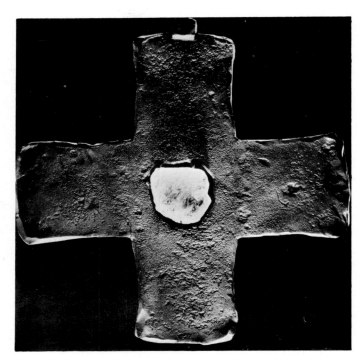

PLATE 188. WROUGHT IRON FREE-STANDING CROSS,
CRYSTAL INSET, 7½ FT. HIGH (2.3 M.), BY FRANZ JOSEF
PETERS, STOLBERG

(FACING) PLATE 189. WROUGHT IRON
LATTICE, WERKKUNSTSCHULE, AACHEN

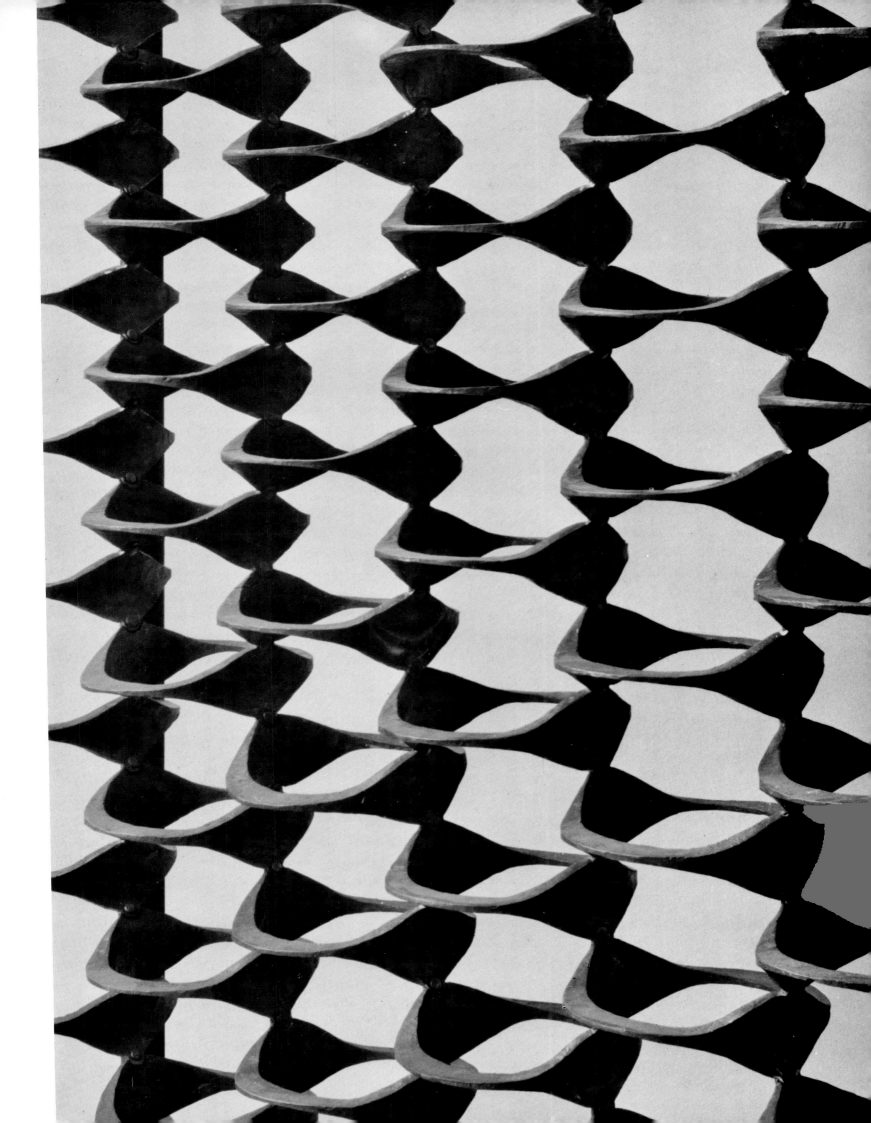

PLATE 190. STONEWARE VASE, 13 IN. HIGH (33 CM.),
BY BERNARD LEACH, ST. IVES

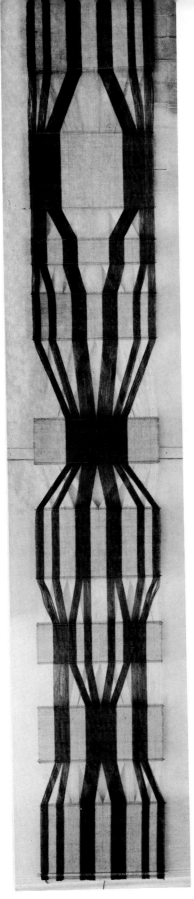

PLATE 191. "MACROGAUZE #7," WOVEN
LINEN HANGING, 10 X 1⅓ FT. (3.05 X .43
M.), BY PETER COLLINGWOOD, NAYLAND,
EAST ANGLIA

PLATE 192. "OVER ALL," TAPESTRY,
5⅓ X 5⅓ FT. (1.62 X 1.62 M.), BY HAROLD
COHEN, LONDON; EXECUTED BY EDIN-
BURGH TAPESTRY COMPANY

(FACING) PLATE 193. PORCELAIN BOWL BY LUCY RIE, LONDON

PLATE 194. "MARINE FORM," THROWN AND COIL-BUILT STONEWARE, 17 X 11 IN. (43 X 28 CM.), BY DEREK DAVIS, ARUNDEL

PLATE 195. CERAMIC FORM, 5 X 8 IN. (12.5 X 20 CM.), BY BRYAN NEWMAN, LONDON

(RIGHT HAND COLUMN)

PLATE 196. CERAMIC VASE, 10 IN. HIGH (25 CM.), BY COLIN JONES, LONDON

PLATE 197. SLAB-BUILT CERAMIC FORM, 10 IN. HIGH (25 CM.), BY ANTHONY HEPBURN, WELWYN

PLATE 198. STONEWARE FORM, COIL BUILT, 12 IN. LONGEST DIMENSION (30.5 CM.), BY EILEEN LOWENSTEIN, LONDON

PLATE 199. SPACE DISC, KNITTED STRING WITH SILVER POLYURETHANE FINISH, 16 IN. DIAM. (41 CM.), BY ANN SUTTON, BANBURY

PLATE 200. CAST SILVER NECKLACE BY GILLIAN PACKARD, LONDON

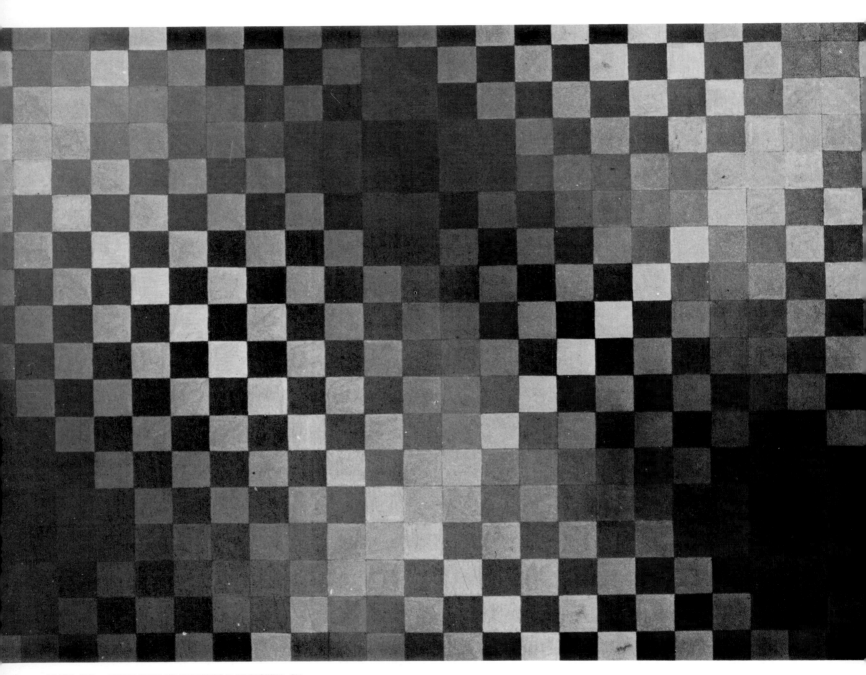

PLATE 201. "HARMONY IN SQUARES," TAPESTRY, 8½
FT. SQUARE (2.3 M.), BY EDUARDO NERY

PLATE 202. "FEMME," CERAMIC, 38 X 21 X 13 IN.
(98 X 54 X 35 CM.), BY JOAN MIRO AND JOSEPH
ARTIGAS, BARCELONA

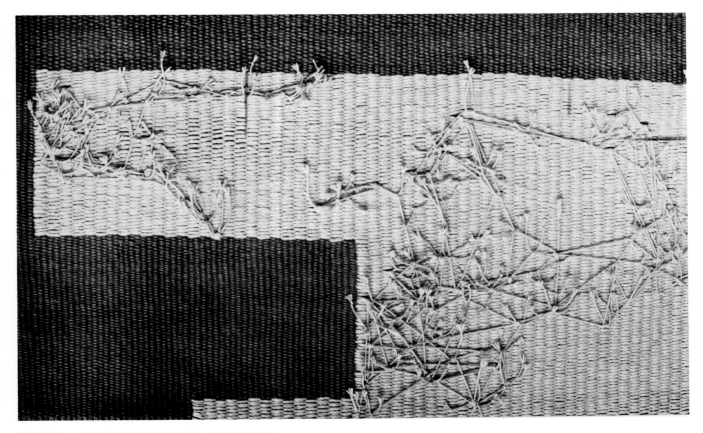

PLATE 203. "WHITE RHYTHM," DETAIL OF TAPESTRY,
10 X 6½ FT. (3. X 2 M.), BY MARIE THERESE CODINA

PLATE 204. BOOKBINDING BY EMILE BRUGALLA,
BARCELONA

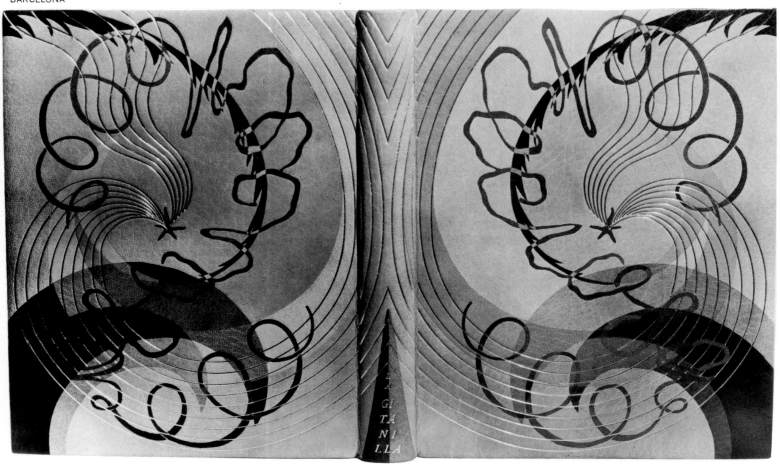

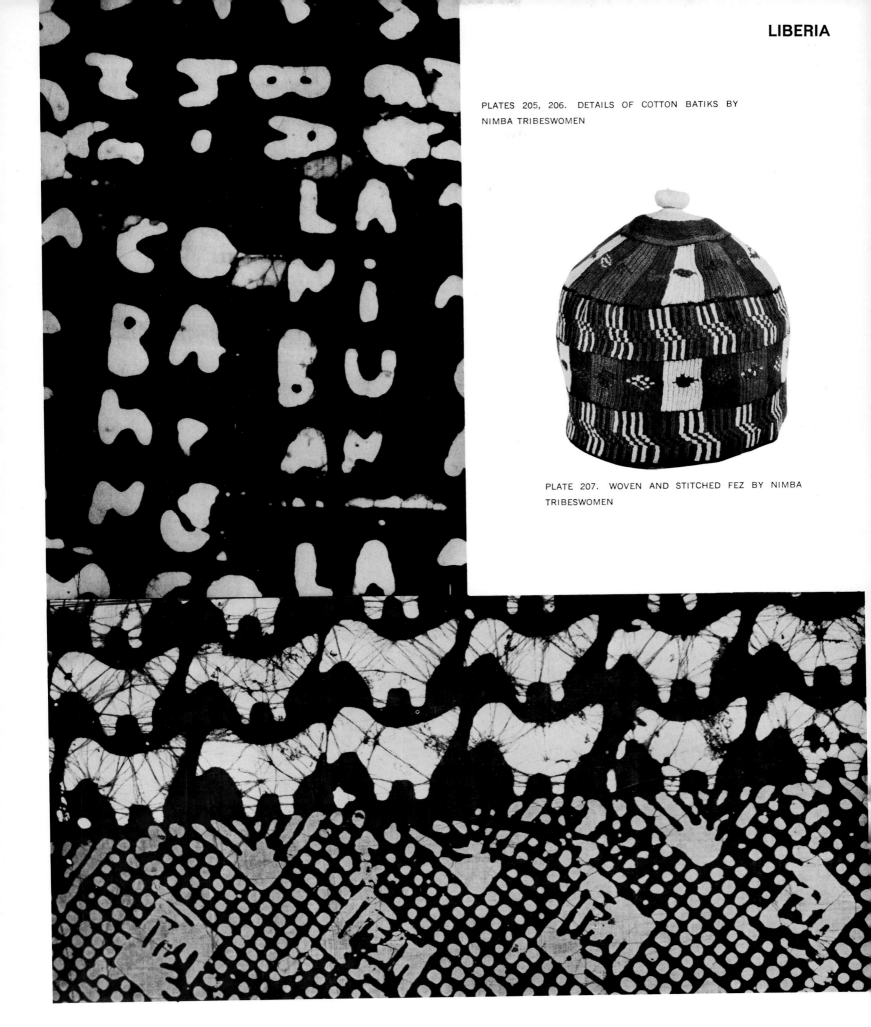

PLATES 205, 206. DETAILS OF COTTON BATIKS BY NIMBA TRIBESWOMEN

PLATE 207. WOVEN AND STITCHED FEZ BY NIMBA TRIBESWOMEN

PLATE 208. BASKET, 14 IN. DIAM. (36 CM.), KUMASI REGION

PLATE 209. COTTON BAND WEAVING, 6 IN. WIDE (15 CM.), KUMASI REGION

PLATES 210, 211. FACADE OF CONCRETE HOUSE DECORATED IN RE-
LIEF, AND DETAIL SHOWING BICYCLE, SWORD AND AIRPLANE MOTIFS
IN ZARIA

PLATE 212. SCULPTURED CEMENT WALL OF ESSO STATION BY
ADEBISI AT OSHOGBO

PLATE 214. SISAL SNAKE, 30 IN. (76 CM.)

PLATE 215. JAR, ABUJA POTTERY

PLATE 213. CARVED WOOD DOLLS FOR EXPORT, 12 AND
8½ IN. HIGH (30 AND 22 CM.), BENIN CITY

PLATES 217 TO 221. *SHAI* POTTERY-MAKING BY WOMEN MASTER-POTTERS OF THE VILLAGE OF DOWODA NEAR ACCRA. THIS COOKING AND STORAGE WARE IS COIL BUILT, SMOOTHED WITH ROCK, AND TEXTURED WITH A DRIED CORN COB. IT IS LOW FIRED OVER BURNING CORN COBS, TWIGS, AND PALM STALKS IN A CRIB-LIKE PIT OF PALM FROND BUTTS, THEN OXIDIZED BLACK BY PILING DAMP LEAVES ON THE POT.

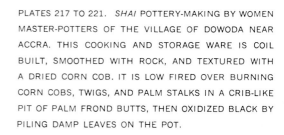

PLATE 222. WOOD CARVING, YORUBA
PLATE 223. BEATEN BRONZE ELEPHANT, 6 IN. HIGH (15 CM.)

PLATE 224.   RAFFIA MAT, PILE WEAVE

PLATE 225.   EARTHENWARE WATER OR MILK JAR,

12 IN. HIGH (31 CM.), BAJOKWE REGION

PLATE 226. WALKING STICKS, (CENTER) FROM OVAM-
BOLAND, S.W. AFRICA, (RIGHT AND LEFT) FROM
BAROTSE, ZAMBIA

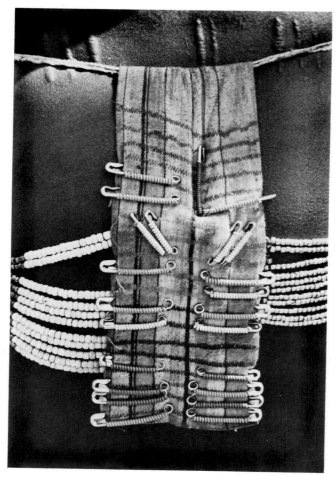

PLATE 227. BEADED AND DECORATED SAFETY PINS ON TRIBAL INITIATION DRESS, VENDA TRIBE, NORTH TRANSVAAL

PLATE 228. BRACELETS AND RINGS, PONDO TRIBE, TRANSKEI

PLATE 229. BRASS ARM AND LEG BANDS ON N'DEBELE BEAD WORKER

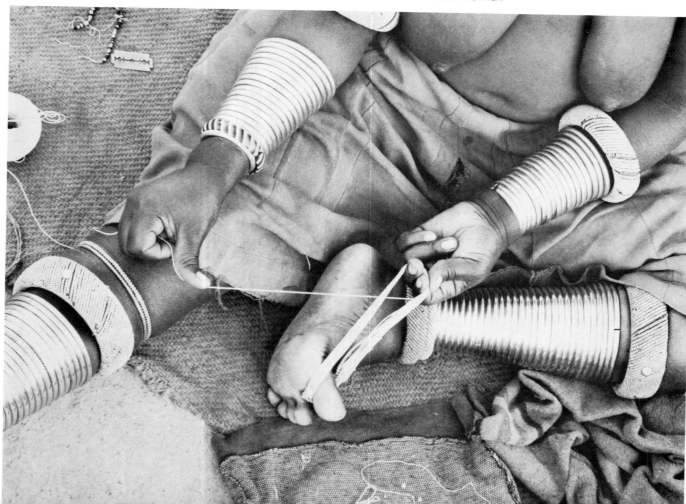

PLATE 230. EARTHENWARE POTS 6½ HIGH (16 TO 50 CM.), SWAZILAND

PLATE 231. "THE FOOTBALL MATCH," WEAVING BY MRS. N'DAWE AT THE EVANGELICAL LUTHERAN CHURCH CRAFT CENTER, RORKES DRIFT, NATAL

PLATE 232. EARTHENWARE WATER POT, VENDA TRIBE, NORTH TRANSVAAL

147

PLATE 233.   PAINTED COURTYARD WALLS
BY N'DEBELE WOMEN NEAR PRETORIA

PLATE 234.   CARVED WOOD GRAVE MARKER

PLATE 235.   DETAIL OF BEADED LEATHER SKIRT BY WAMBULU TRIBESWOMAN

PLATE 237. CERAMIC JAR, 10 IN. HIGH (25 CM.), BY
MOHAMED TAHA HUSSEIN, GIZA

PLATE 236. WOOD MASK, 41 IN. HIGH (104 CM.),
DOGON REGION

PLATE 238. DETAIL OF WEAVING BY CHILDREN UNDER
THE DIRECTION OF RAMSES WISSA WASSEF, GIZA

PLATE 239. OLIVE WOOD KOHL APPLICATOR FROM DJERBA

PLATE 240. SILVER CHAIN WITH HAND OF *FATIMA*, BERBER

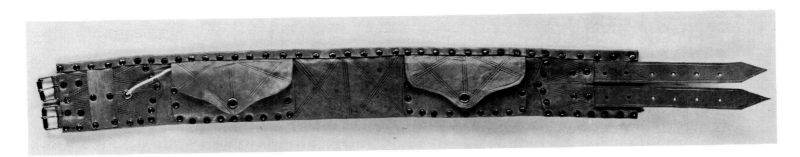

PLATE 241. TOOLED GOAT LEATHER MONEY BELT

PLATE 242.   CERAMIC OIL LAMPS FROM THE KABYLIA MOUNTAINS

PLATE 243. FIBULA, SILVER WITH ENAMELLED SILVER
AND CORAL PENDANTS

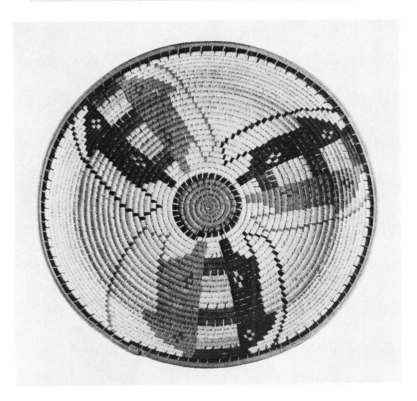

PLATE 244. BASKET, 12 IN. DIAM. (30.5 CM.)

PLATE 245. BRASS ALLIGATOR, TOOLED AND ENAMELLED, 6 IN. LONG (15 CM.)

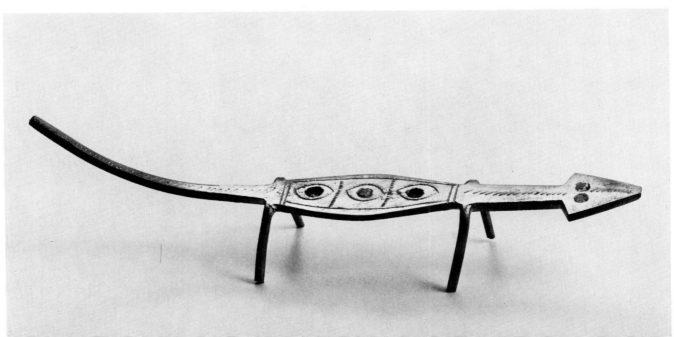

155

PLATE 246. EMBROIDERED WOVEN COVER FROM MARRAKECH

PLATE 247. BERBER WOOL RUG FROM MIDDLE ATLAS MOUNTAINS

PLATE 248.   THROWN CERAMIC FORM, 2½ FT. HIGH
(.76 M), BY JOHN R. JORDAN, CALIFORNIA

PLATE 249. STONEWARE PLATE, CONSTRUCTED AND THROWN, 17 IN. DIAM. (43 CM.), BY PETER VOULKOS, CALIFORNIA

(FACING) PLATE 250. CERAMIC POTS, THROWN AND PAINTED WITH GLAZES 10 TO 21 IN. HIGH (25 TO 53 CM.), BY HUI KA KWONG, NEW YORK. SILK-SCREENED TEXTILE BY KEN SCOTT, MILAN, ITALY

(TOP) PLATE 252. STONEWARE COVERED JAR, 24 IN.
DIAM. (61 CM.), BY NAN MCKINNELL, NEW YORK

(BOTTOM) PLATE 253. STONEWARE FORM, 7½ IN.
HIGH (19 CM.), BY TISHIKO TAKAEZU, NEW JERSEY

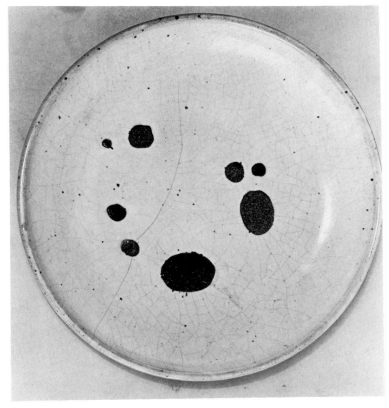

(TOP) PLATE 254. STONEWARE PLATE, 17 IN. DIAM. (43
CM.), BY HENRY LIN, OHIO

(BOTTOM) PLATE 255. CERAMIC CHRYSANTHEMUM
POT, 13 IN. HIGH (33 CM.), BY MARY RISLEY, CONNECTI-
CUT

PLATE 251. FREE-STANDING WOVEN FORM, HEMP
WRAPPED WITH WOOL, 21 X 13 IN. (53 X 33 CM.), BY
CLAIRE ZEISLER, ILLINOIS

161

PLATE 256. CERAMIC JAR WITH HANDLES, 30 X 34 IN.
(76 X 86 CM.), BY JERRY ROTHMAN, CALIFORNIA

PLATE 257. "EYE POT," THROWN PORCELAIN WITH
SGRAFFITO DECORATION, 7 IN. HIGH (18 CM.), BY
RUDOLF STAFFEL, PENNSYLVANIA

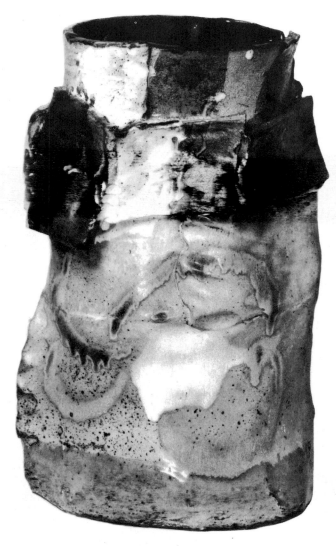

PLATE 258. STONEWARE VASE, 18½ IN. HIGH (47 CM.),
BY RUDY AUTIO, MONTANA

PLATE 259. CERAMIC FORM, 5 FT. HIGH (1.52 M.), BY
JOHN MASON, CALIFORNIA

PLATE 260. CERAMIC POT, PHOTO DECAL, 18 IN.
HIGH (46 CM.), BY ROBERT ENGLE, OHIO

PLATE 261. "BRUCE," STONEWARE, 7½ X 23 IN. (19 X
58 CM.), BY JOSEPH PUGLIESE, CALIFORNIA

PLATE 262. "ELEPHANT FOOT OTTOMAN #2," EARTH-
ENWARE WITH SYNTHETIC LEOPARD FUR, 8½ X 21
IN. (22 X 53 CM.), BY DAVID GILHOOLY, CALIFORNIA

(TOP) PLATE 264. "CHECKERED GHOST," CERAMIC, 8
IN. HIGH (20 CM.), BY JAMES MELCHERT, CALIFORNIA
(BOTTOM) PLATE 265. "HOMAGE TO ROBERT FROST,"
STONEWARE, 30 IN. HIGH (76 CM.), BY WILLIAM WYMAN,
MASSACHUSETTS

PLATE 263. STONEWARE PLATE, 2½ X 15 IN. (6 X 38
CM.), BY ERIK GRONBORG, OREGON

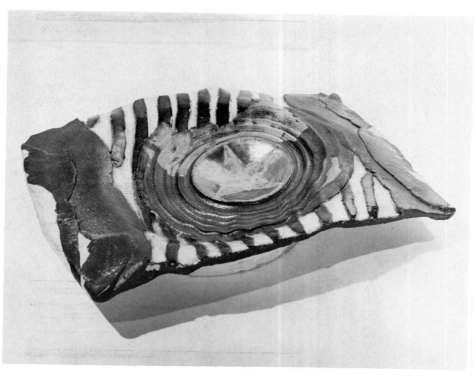

(TOP) PLATE 266. CERAMIC FLOOR POT, 24 IN. HIGH (61 CM.), BY FRANZ WILDENHAIN, NEW YORK

(BOTTOM) PLATE 267. CERAMIC FIREPLACE, COIL- AND SLAB-BUILT, FIREBOX, 3 FT. HIGH (92 CM.), BY KAREN KARNES, NEW YORK

(TOP) PLATE 268. CERAMIC VASE, 8 IN. HIGH (20 CM.), BY MAIJA GROTELL, MICHIGAN

(BOTTOM) PLATE 269. STONEWARE POT, CRATER GLAZE, BY GERTRUD AND OTTO NATZLER, CALIFORNIA

(TOP) PLATE 272. CERAMIC BOTTLE, 8 IN. HIGH (20 CM.), BY JAMES WOZNIAK, ILLINOIS

(BOTTOM) PLATE 273. CERAMIC POTS THROWN AND DISTORTED, 25 IN. HIGH (64 CM.), BY DONALD MARCH, MICHIGAN

(TOP) PLATE 270. STONEWARE PLANTER BY SUSAN PETERSON, CALIFORNIA

(BOTTOM) PLATE 271. STONEWARE BOTTLE BY MARY NYBURG, MARYLAND

(RIGHT) PLATE 274. STONEWARE VASE, SLAB CON-
STRUCTED, 31 IN. HIGH (79 CM.), BY WIN NG, CALI-
FORNIA

(BOTTOM) PLATE 275. RAKU PLATTER WITH INLAID
CLAY, 12 X 18 IN. (30 X 46 CM.), BY PAUL SOLDNER,
COLORADO

PLATE 276. WALL RELIEF, STONEWARE AND ACRYLIC,
16 IN. HIGH (41 CM.), BY KEN SHORES, OREGON

PLATE 277. "ALL AMERICAN," CERAMIC TROPHY, 25
IN. HIGH (64 CM.), BY ROBERT ARNESON, CALIFORNIA

(RIGHT) PLATE 278. WOVEN WOOL HANGING, 11¾ X 5 IN. (30 X 13 CM.), BY SHEILA HICKS, KANSAS, NOW WORKING IN PARIS

(BOTTOM) PLATE 279. "OP BANNER," WOVEN SILK, 18 X 24 IN. (46 X 61 CM.), BY TRUDE GUERMONPREZ, CALIFORNIA

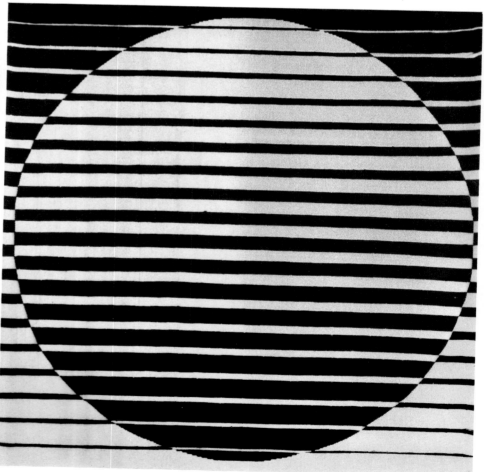

(FACING TOP) PLATE 280. TRIPLE WEAVE WALL HANG-
ING, 82 X 47 IN. (208 X 120 CM.), BY ANNI ALBERS,
CONNECTICUT

(LEFT) PLATE 281. WOOL TAPESTRY, 40 X 28¾ IN. (102
X 73 CM.), BY AHZA COHEN, NEW YORK

(RIGHT) PLATE 282. "PHASE," WOOL TAPESTRY, 54 X
54 IN. (137 X 137 CM.), BY SUSAN WEITZMAN, NEW YORK

PLATE 283. CROCHET WOOL CONSTRUCTION ON WIRE
FRAME, 29 DIAM. X 7 IN. DEEP (74 X 18 CM.), BY RON
GOODMAN, CALIFORNIA

PLATE 284. "A JEWEL IN THE GRASS," TAPESTRY OF
PAPER AND METAL, 25 X 22 IN. (64 X 56 CM.), BY NELL
ZNAMIEROWSKI, NEW YORK

PLATE 285. BASKET, RAFFIA INTERLACED AND WRAP-
PED OVER WIRE FRAME, 12 X 11 IN. (31 X 28 CM.), BY
ED ROSSBACH, CALIFORNIA

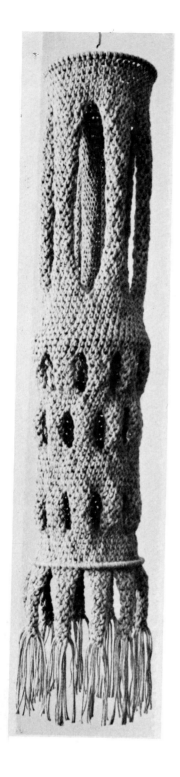

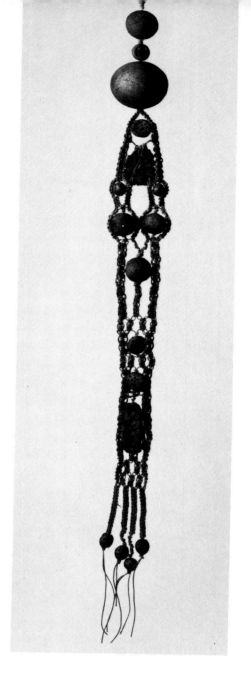

(LEFT) PLATE 286. "INTROSPECTION," FORM OF LINEN
ON STEEL FRAME, 62 LONG X 9 IN. DIAM. (157 X 23
CM.), BY GLEN KAUFMAN, MICHIGAN
(CENTER) PLATE 287. KNITTED FORM OF BRASS AND
COPPER WIRE, 96 HIGH X 18 IN. DIAM. (244 X 46 CM.),
BY RUTH ASAWA, CALIFORNIA
(RIGHT) PLATE 288. MACRAME HANGING BY MARY
WALKER PHILLIPS, NEW YORK; CONSTRUCTED AROUND
RAKU POTS BY CHARLES BROWN, FLORIDA

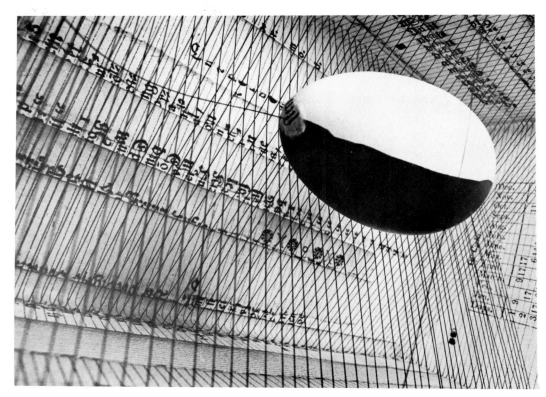

PLATE 289. "THE GOLDEN NUMBER," BOXED CONSTRUCTION OF PAPER, EGG, AND THREADS, 7 X 4 IN. (18 X 10 CM.), BY LENORE TAWNEY, NEW YORK

PLATE 290. "FANTASIA," WOOL PANEL, CROCHETED, STITCHED, INTERWOVEN, AND KNOTTED, 16½ X 21 IN. (42 X 53 CM.), BY KATE AUERBACH, NEW YORK

PLATE 291. "UNCLE BOB," ASSEMBLAGE OF OBJECTS AND STITCHERY, 34 X 21 IN. (86 X 53 CM.), BY ALMA LESCH, KENTUCKY

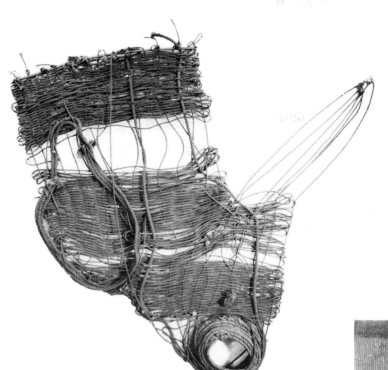

PLATE 292. WOVEN RELIEF, TARRED ROPE AND IRON
BAR, 5-5/6 X 3⅔ FT. (1.77 X 1.12 M.), BY ALICE ADAMS,
NEW YORK

PLATE 293. TAPESTRY, HAND-DYED WOOL WITH RYA
AND FLOSSA KNOTS, 4⅔ X 2¾ FT. (1.40 X 84 M.), BY
ALICE PARROTT, NEW MEXICO

(LEFT) PLATE 294. HANGING, TIE-DYE WARP, 8 X 2⅔ FT. (2.28 X 1.32 M.), BY KAREN CHANG, MARYLAND

(BOTTOM) PLATE 295. "WATER LILIES," DETAIL OF BATIK, 50 IN. WIDE (127 CM.), BY JACK LENOR LARSEN, NEW YORK

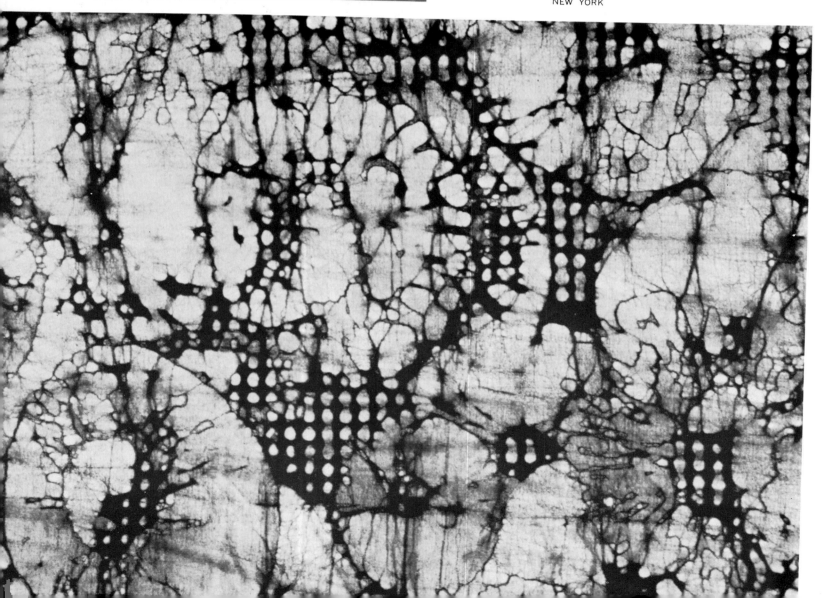

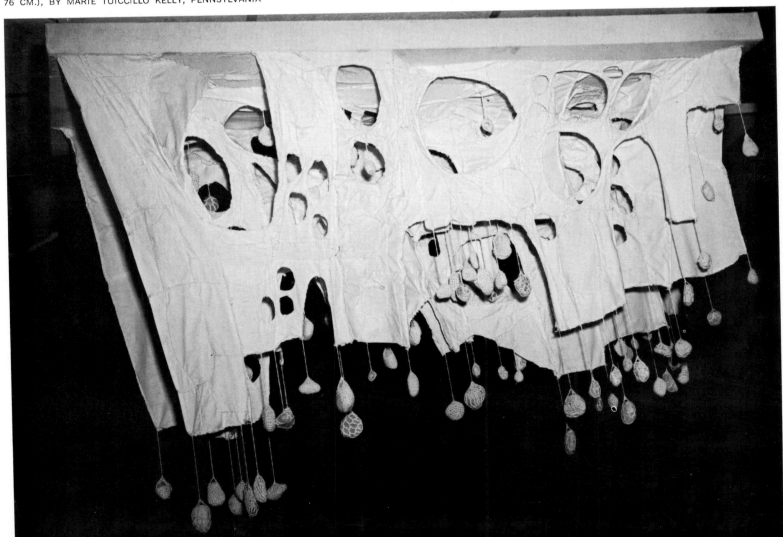

(RIGHT) PLATE 296. HANGING, MULTI-LAYER NYLON MONOFILAMENT WEAVE, 40 IN. LONG (102 CM.), BY KAY SEKIMACHI, CALIFORNIA

(BOTTOM) PLATE 297. "WHITE BANNER," STITCHED CONSTRUCTION, MUSLIN AND STRING WITH PEBBLES IN CROCHETED SACKS, 60 X 20 X 30 IN. (152 X 51 X 76 CM.), BY MARIE TUICCILLO KELLY, PENNSYLVANIA

PLATE 298.   BLOWN GLASS FORM, 4 X 8½ IN. (10 X 22 CM.), BY HARVEY LITTLETON, WISCONSIN

PLATE 299. "HERC," BLOWN GLASS FORM WITH BRONZE AND WOOD, 20 X 30 IN. (51 X 76 CM.), BY JAMES WAYNE, CALIFORNIA

PLATE 300. BOTTLE, BLOWN AND PRUNTED, 13 IN. HIGH (33 CM.), BY JOHN BURTON, CALIFORNIA

PLATE 302. BLOWN GLASS FORM, 10 IN. HIGH (25.5 CM.), BY DOMINIC LABINO, OHIO

PLATE 301. BLOWN GLASS VASE, 5½ IN. HIGH (14 CM.), BY STEVEN MILDWOFF, NEW YORK

PLATE 303. BLOWN GLASS BOTTLE, PARTIALLY FORMED ON THE SURFACE OF A PATTERNED ALUMINUM SLAB, 7 IN. HIGH (18 CM.), BY JOEL MYERS, WEST VIRGINIA

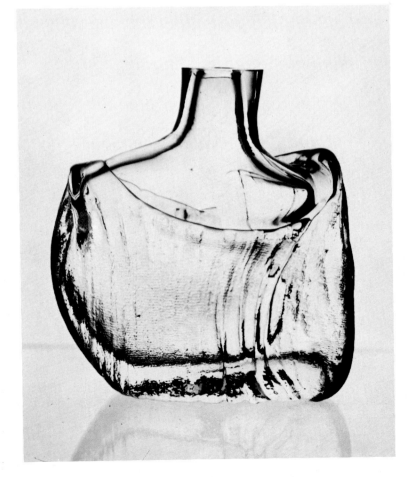

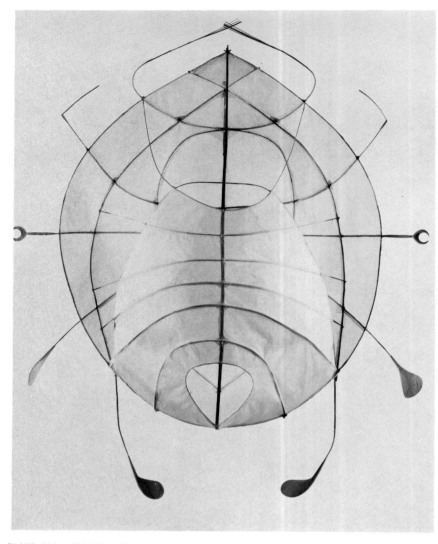

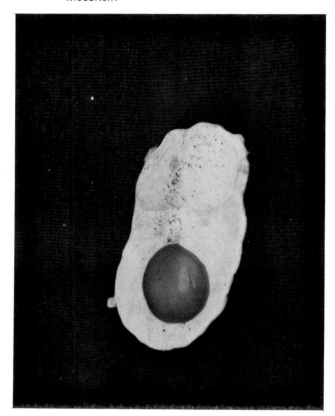

PLATE 305. FRIED EGG NIGHT LIGHT, NEON AND PLASTIC, 4 X 6 IN. (10 X 15 CM.), BY CLAYTON BAILEY, WISCONSIN

PLATE 304. "LOUSE," *SEKI-SHU* PAPER ON BAMBOO FRAME, 39½ LONG X 32 WIDE X 13¼ IN. DEEP (100 X 81 X 34 CM.), BY FUMIO YOSHIMURA, NEW YORK

PLATE 306. PLASTIC BRACELET BY CARLOS SANSE-GUNDO, NEW YORK

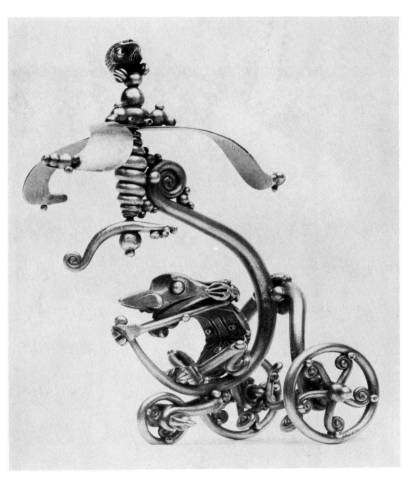

PLATE 307. "THE AIR MACHINE #6,"
CAST SILVER, 7 IN. HIGH (18 CM.), BY
BRENT KINGTON, ILLINOIS

PLATE 308. "COME ALIVE, YOU'RE IN
THE PEPSI GENERATION," BADGE OF
MIXED METALS, 4 X 4 IN. (10 X 10 CM.),
BY FRED WOELL, MICHIGAN

PLATE 309. SILVER TEAPOT, EBONY FIN-
IAL AND RATTAN HANDLE, 7 IN. HIGH
(18 CM.), BY JOHN PRIP, MASSACHU-
SETTS

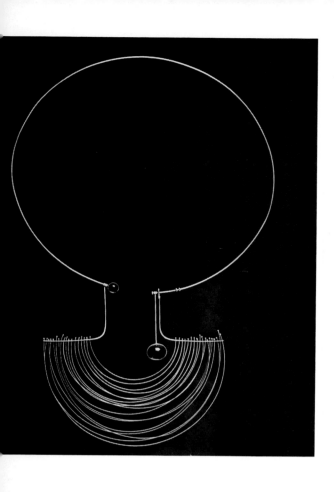

PLATE 310. GOLD NECKLACE WITH AME-
THYSTS BY JOHN SNIDECOR, CALIFORNIA

PLATE 311. "ROBBERY," NECKLACE OF
FOUND OBJECTS, BY TAMARA KARLA
SURENDORF

PLATE 312. SILVER INCENSE BOX WITH
FILIGREE INSERTS BY HELLYN MOOR,
WASHINGTON

PLATE 313. SILVER BRACELET BY RON-
ALD PEARSON, NEW YORK

PLATE 314. RING, CAST GOLD WITH TOPAZ AND PEARL, BY BOB WINSTON, ARIZONA

PLATE 315. FORGED SILVER HANDPIECE BY SUSAN LONG, CALIFORNIA

PLATE 316. SILVER NECKLACE BY LINDA WATSON, CALIFORNIA

PLATE 317. GOLD PIN WITH QUARTZ AND CRYSTAL BY HEIKKI SEPPA, KENTUCKY

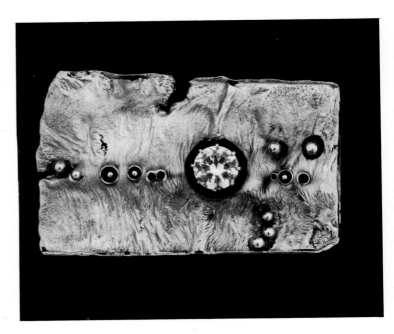

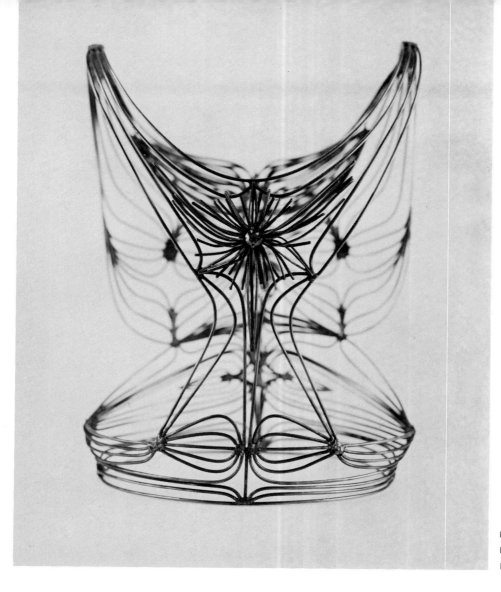

PLATE 318. "IRON MAIDEN," WROUGHT IRON WITH PEARLS, SAPPHIRES, AND PERIDOT, BY ROBERT DHAEMERS, CALIFORNIA

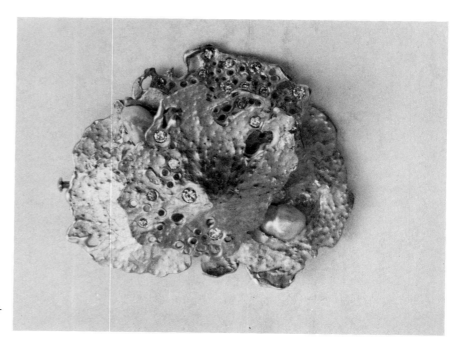

PLATE 319. CAST GOLD PIN WITH PEARLS AND PRECIOUS STONES BY IRENA BRYNNER, NEW YORK

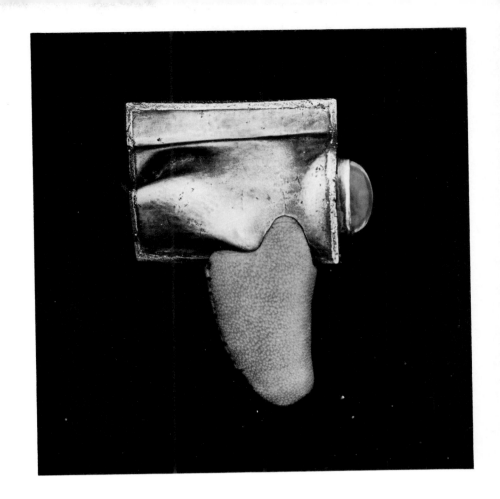

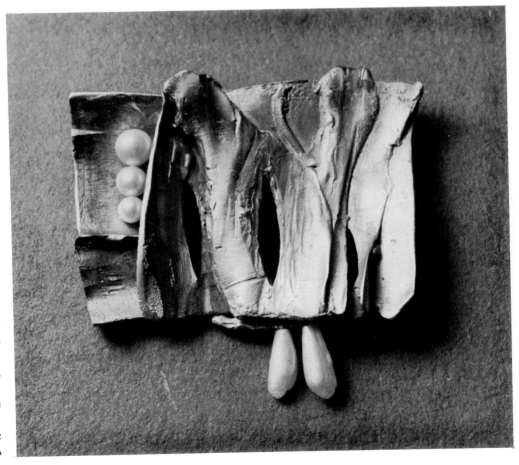

(TOP LEFT) PLATE 320. ELECTROFORMED PIN WITH SILVER GILT AND TOURMALINE CRYSTAL, BY STANLEY LECHTZIN, PENNSYLVANIA

(TOP RIGHT) PLATE 321. PIN OF SILVER, LEATHER, AND STONE BY KEN CORY, WASHINGTON

(BOTTOM LEFT) PLATE 322. SILVER AND BRASS PIN BY RAY HEIN, CALIFORNIA

(BOTTOM RIGHT) PLATE 323. GOLD-PLATED SILVER PIN WITH PEARLS BY OLAF SKOOGFORS, PENNSYLVANIA

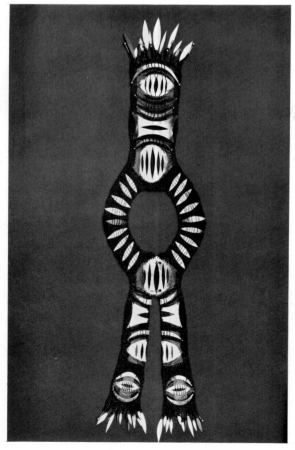

(TOP) PLATE 324. PAINTED PAPIER-MACHE NECKLACE BY CHRYSTYA OLENSKA, NEW YORK
(BOTTOM) PLATE 325. WOVEN NECKLACE OF WOOL WITH SILVER, 39 IN. LONG (99 CM.), BY ARLINE FISCH, CALIFORNIA

(FACING) PLATE 326. WALNUT LIBRARY LADDER, 48 X 18 X 27 IN. (122 X 46 X 69 CM.), BY WHARTON ESHERICK, PENNSYLVANIA
PLATE 327. OAK CHAIR WITH LEATHER, 45 X 48 IN. (114 X 122 CM.), BY WENDELL CASTLE, NEW YORK
PLATE 328. LAMINATED ASH DESK WITH NYLON PILE SEAT, 40 IN. HIGH (102 CM.), BY ROBIN STEWART METZE, CALIFORNIA

(LEFT) PLATE 329. PANEL, ENAMEL ON WOOD, 13 X 10 IN. (33 X 25 CM.), BY JUNE SCHWARCZ, CALIFORNIA (BELOW) PLATE 330. MODEL FOR A HOLLOW, FREE-STANDING WALL, ENAMEL ON COPPER, 3 X 12 X 1 FT. (1.50 X 3 X .28 M.), BY PAUL HULTBERG, NEW YORK

PLATE 331. ENAMELLED COPPER FORM BY VIVIAN KOOS, NEW YORK
(BELOW) PLATE 332. STAINED GLASS WINDOW, TEMPLE MISHKAN TEFILA, NEWTON, MASSACHUSETTS, BY ROBERT SOWERS, NEW YORK

(TOP) PLATE 333. MOSAIC OF WEATHERED WOOD AND TILE, 40 X 34 IN. (102 X 86 CM.), BY GLEN MICHAELS, MICHIGAN

(BOTTOM) PLATE 334. "ONE DIVIDED BY ONE," MARBLE MOSAIC PANEL, 24 X 24 IN. (61 X 61 CM.), BY ALEXANDRA KASUBA, NEW YORK

(TOP) PLATE 335. "SWAN WAYS," MOTHER-OF-PEARL AND PUMICE STONE SET IN CEMENT, 5 X 6 FT. (1.5 X 1.8 M.), BY JEANNE REYNAL, NEW YORK

(BOTTOM) PLATE 336. PLASTIC SCREEN BY FREDA KOBLICK, CALIFORNIA

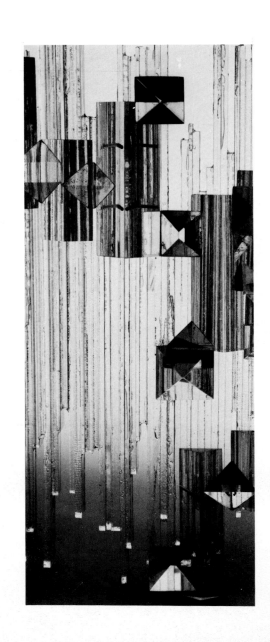

190

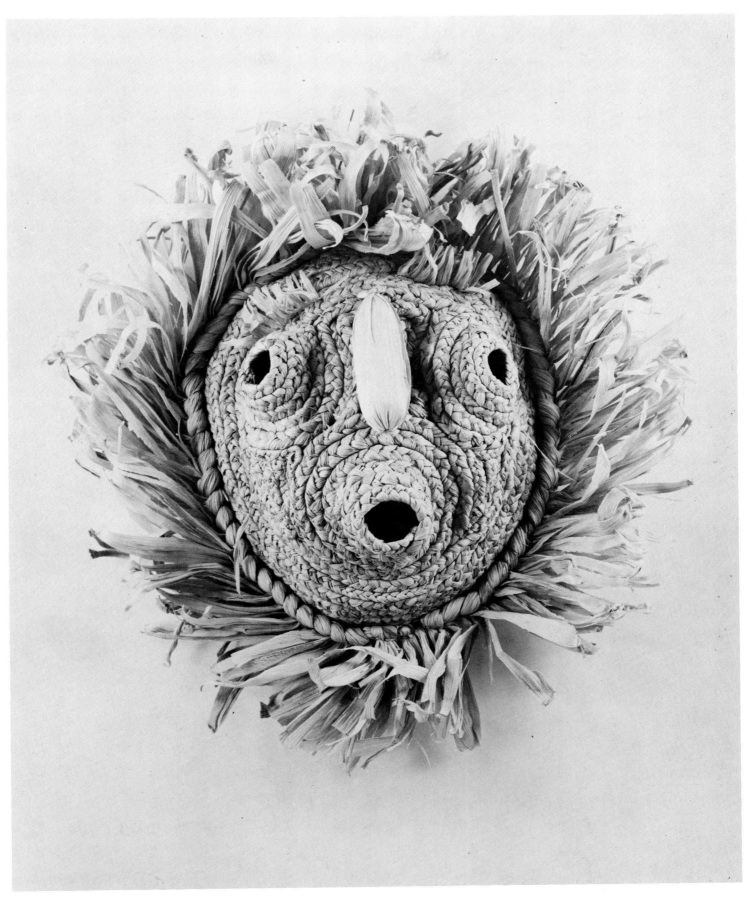

PLATE 337.   BRAIDED CORN HUSK MASK, 14 IN. HIGH
(36 CM.), IROQUOIS INDIAN, NEW YORK

PLATE 338.   BEADED BOTTLE, 11 IN. HIGH (28 CM.),
PAIUTE INDIAN, PYRAMID LAKE, NEVADA

PLATE 339.   WOVEN SADDLE BLANKET, NAVAJO INDIAN, ARIZONA

PLATE 340. PLAITED RIVER CANE MAT, 59 X 47 IN. (150 X 119.5 CM.), CHOCTAW INDIAN, MISSISSIPPI

PLATE 341. BASKET OF HAZLEWOOD ROOT FIBERS DECORATED WITH FEATHERS, 3 IN. DIAM., (7.5 CM.), PIMA INDIAN, CALIFORNIA

PLATE 342. BASKET, DYED AND NATURAL RIVER CANE,
17¼ IN. (44 CM.), BY LIZZIE YOUNGBIRD, CHEROKEE
INDIAN, NORTH CAROLINA

PLATE 343. EARTHENWARE POT, PAINTED SLIP, 8¼ IN.
HIGH (21 CM.), BY LUCY LEWIS, PUEBLO, NEW MEXICO

PLATE 344.   BUILT POT, SLIP DECORATION, 6 IN. HIGH
(15 CM.), BY LUCY LEWIS, PUEBLO INDIAN, NEW MEXICO

(FACING) PLATE 345.   DOUBLE WEAVE WOOL SADDLE
BLANKET, 57 X 30 IN. (145 X 77 CM.), BY LUCY WILSON,
NAVAJO INDIAN, ARIZONA

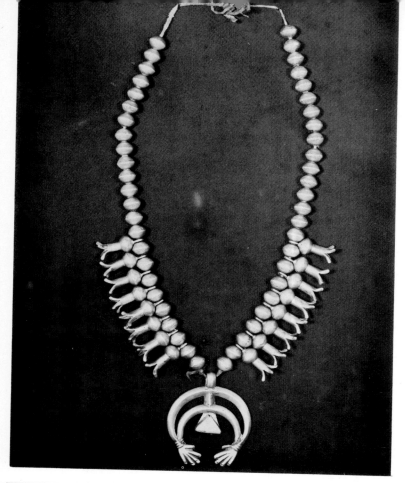

PLATE 346. SILVER NECKLACE, 15 IN. LONG (38 CM.), NAVAJO INDIAN, NEW MEXICO
PLATE 347. PORCUPINE OF NAILS IN WOOD MADE AT THE INSTITUTE OF AMERICAN INDIAN CULTURE, SANTA FE, NEW MEXICO

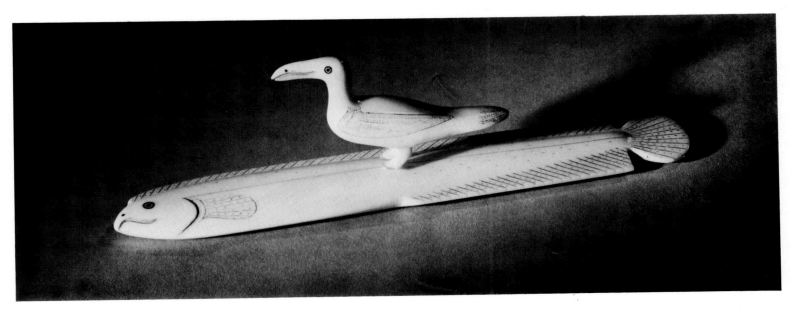

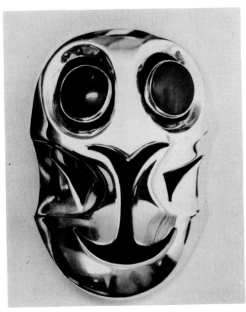

PLATE 348. IVORY BIRD AND FISH, CARVED AND ENGRAVED, 6⅛ IN. HIGH (15 CM.), ESKIMO, ALASKA

PLATE 349. SILVER PIN SET WITH JADE, 2⅜ IN. HIGH (6 CM.), BY JAMES OKPEALUK, ESKIMO, ALASKA

PLATE 350. SILVER BRACELET INLAID WITH JADE AND IVORY BY JERRY NORTON, ESKIMO, ALASKA

PLATE 351. RAVEN MASK, CARVED WALNUT WITH INLAID REDWOOD, 9 IN. HIGH (23 CM.), BY ANTHONY PUSHRUK, ESKIMO, ALASKA

PLATE 352. "BEAR ATTACKING WALRUS," CARVED
SOAPSTONE BY PAULOSSIE OF POVUNGNETUK, ESKIMO
PLATE 353. "SNOWY OWL," CARVED SOAPSTONE, ES-
KIMO, EASTERN ARCTIC

PLATE 354. CERAMIC POTS (LEFT TO RIGHT):
JACK SURES, SASKATCHEWAN
JAN AND HELGA GROVE, BRITISH COLUMBIA
MAYTA MARKSON, ONTARIO
FRANCES HATFIELD, BRITISH COLUMBIA
GERALD TILLAPAUGH, MANITOBA
ED DRAHANCHUK, ALBERTA

PLATE 355. CERAMIC POTS BY DAVID LONG, PHOTO-
GRAPHS ON SURFACE BY WiLLY CADOT, ONTARIO

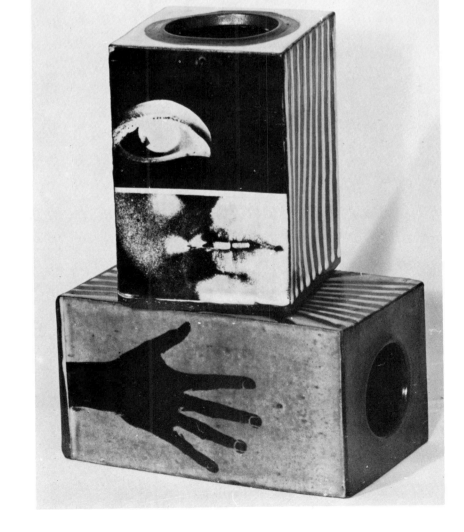

PLATE 356. THROWN STONEWARE FLOOR POT, 28 IN. HIGH (71 CM.), BY JOAN BOBBS, ONTARIO; THROWN MINIATURE POT, 3½ IN. HIGH (9 CM.), BY JOHN BOERRIGTER, BRITISH COLUMBIA

PLATE 357. STONEWARE VASES BY WALTER DROHAN, ALBERTA

(LEFT) PLATE 358. WOVEN HANGING BY CHARLOTTE LINDGREN, NOVA SCOTIA

(BELOW) PLATE 359. TAPESTRY, WOVEN COTTON, FLAX AND PLASTIC BY HELENA BARYNINA, PROVINCE OF QUEBEC

PLATE 360. JEWELED PIN BY VAN YPERIN, BRITISH COLUMBIA

PLATE 361. ENAMEL PANEL BY NORMAN FILLION, PROVINCE OF QUEBEC

PLATE 362. TERRA-COTTA MURAL IN NORTH AMERICAN TOWER, TORONTO, 1383 SQ. FT. (ABOUT 128½ SQ. M.), BY JORDI BONET, PROVINCE OF QUEBEC

(LEFT) PLATE 363. CERAMIC LIDDED POT BY REYNA HERRERA, CARACUS

(CENTER) PLATE 364. CERAMIC FORM AND POT BY SEKA SEVERIN TUDJA, CARACAS

(BOTTOM) PLATE 365. CERAMIC VASE BY THEKLA AND GOTTFRIED ZIELKE, CARACAS

PLATE 366.   GLASS PAPERWEIGHTS BY RUBEN NUNEZ,
CARACAS, FOR ARAYA GLASS FACTORY

PLATE 367.   WOOL RUG FROM HANS NEUMAN, CARACAS

PLATE 368.   BASKET, YEKANA INDIAN

PLATE 369. GOLD PINS BY ROBERTO BURLE MARX, RIO DE JANEIRO

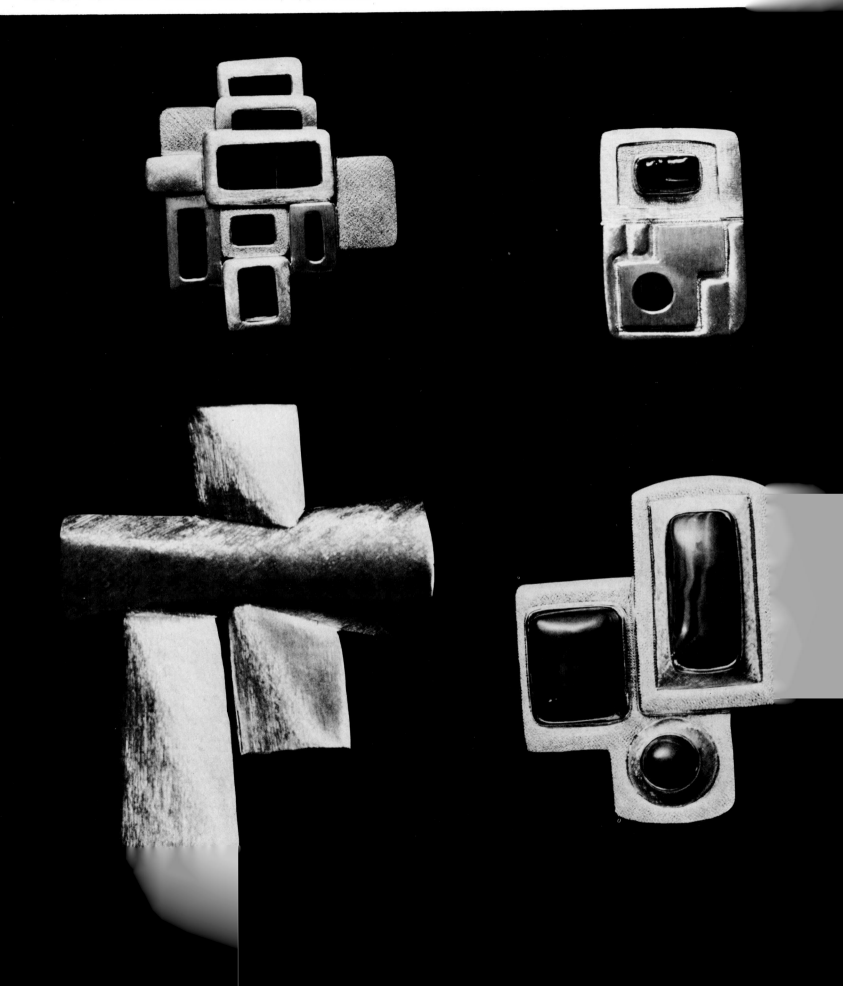

PLATE 370. TAPESTRY BY JACQUES DOUCHEZ, SAO PAULO

PLATE 371. INLAID STONE WALL BY FREDA JARDIM BONDI, RIO DE JANEIRO

PLATE 372. CERAMIC FORM BY PERLA DE BARDIN, BUENOS AIRES

PLATE 373. TAPESTRY BY MARIA MARTORELL, BUENOS AIRES

PLATE 374. "PUEBLO ANDINO," TAPES-TRY BY JOAN WALL, BUENOS AIRES

PLATE 375. "ARBOL DE LA PLAZA LA-VALLE," 3 X 5⅓ FT. (.90 X 1.60 M.), BY GRACIA CUTULI, BUENOS AIRES

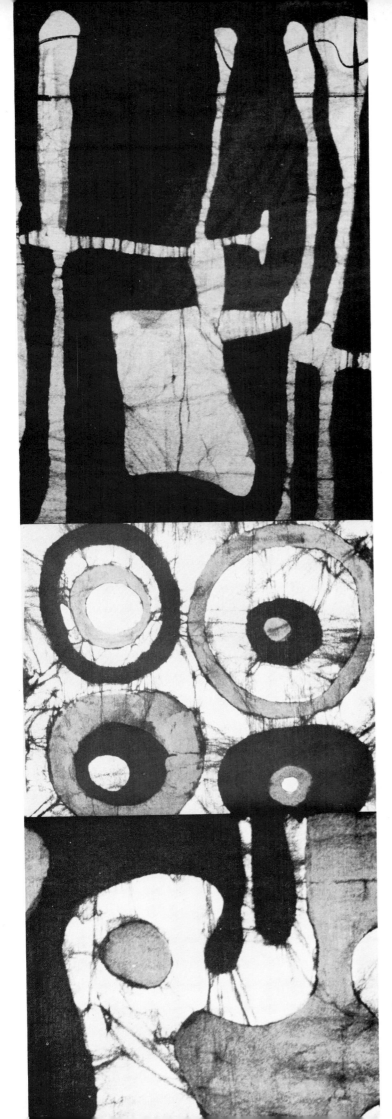

PLATE 376.   DETAILS OF THREE BATIKS BY INGE DUSI, SANTIAGO

PLATE 377. CERAMIC VASE, 24 IN. HIGH (61 CM.),
BY RICARDO YRARRAZAVAL, SANTIAGO

PLATE 378. "PYRAMID," CERAMIC FORM, 17½ IN.
HIGH (45 CM.), BY LUIS MANDIALA, SANTIAGO

PLATE 379. COIN SILVER CUP, 4½ IN. HIGH (11 X 5 CM.), UMBALA AND INCA DESIGNS

PLATE 380. GOLD PIN WITH PEARLS BY NILDA NUNEZ DEL PRADO, LA PAZ

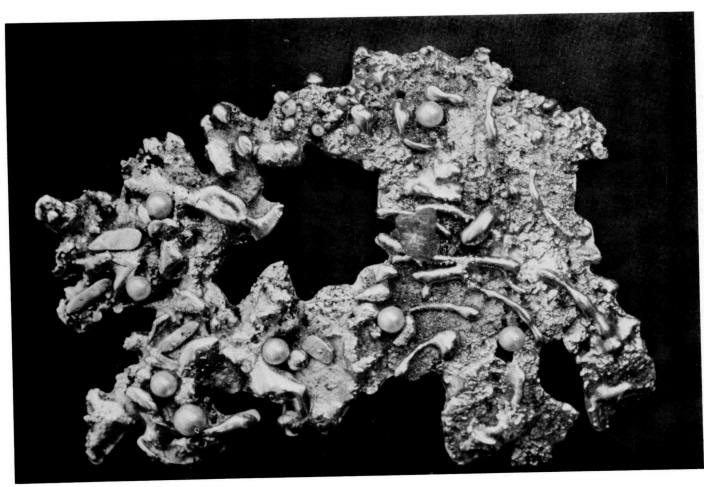

PERU

PLATE 381. CANDLES FROM CUZCO

PLATE 382. CERAMIC FIGURES, BISQUE FIRED AND SLIP PAINTED FROM QUINUA

PLATE 383. COATAHUASI WOOL RUG PRODUCED IN WORKSHOP OF JUAN BLAS AND ANTONIO QUICO-QUICO, AREQUIPA

PLATE 384. DETAIL OF WARP-STRIPED COTTON TEX-
TILE, PAINTED WITH BARK JUICE, BY AMAZON VALLEY
INDIANS.

PLATE 385.   BREAD DOLLS FOR ALL SOULS' DAY, MAN
12 IN. HIGH (30.5 CM.)
PLATE 386.   DETAIL OF WOOL RUG IN U.N. HEAD-
QUARTERS BY OLGA FISCH, QUITO

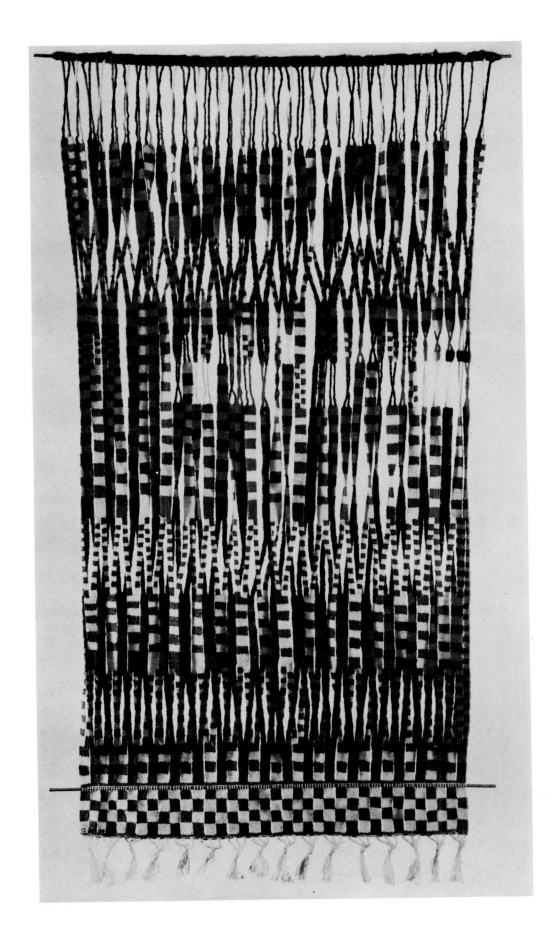

PLATE 387. WOOL HANGING OF BANDS, DOUBLE
WOVEN AND INTERLACED, 49 IN. HIGH (124 CM.),
BY OLGA AMARAL, BOGOTA

PLATE 388, 389. "CANAL 2 TV" AND "TWO BIRDS,"
COTTON APPLIQUES, 14 X 20 IN. (36 X 51 CM.), SAN
BLAS INDIANS

PLATE 390. CARVED WOOD SCARECROW

PLATE 391. COTTON PONCHO AND PANTS BY MAYAN INDIANS

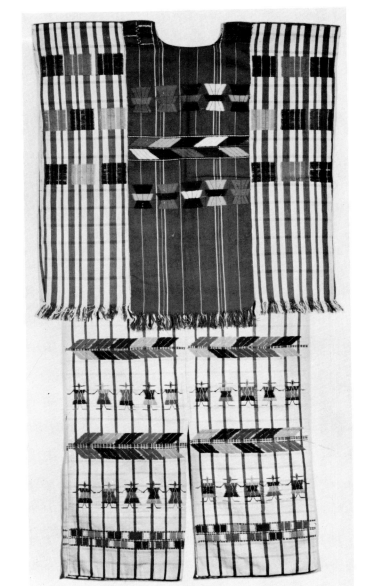

PLATE 392. CERAMIC FIGURE BY THEODORA BLANCO, MEXICO, D.F.

PLATE 393. PAPIER-MACHE SKULL FOR ALL SOULS' DAY

PLATE 394. CHAIR OF NATURAL WOOD, 33½ IN. HIGH (85 CM.), BY PEDRO FRIEDEBERG, MEXICO, D.F.

PLATE 395. BARK PAPER CUTOUT, 9 IN. HIGH (23 CM.), BY OTOMI INDIANS, SIERRA DE PUEBLA

PLATE 396. "IMAGE OF MEXICO," BRONZE COLUMN IN THE NATIONAL MUSEUM OF ANTHROPOLOGY, MEXICO, D.F., 37 FT. HIGH (11 M.), BY JOSE CHAVEZ-MORADO, GUANAJUATO

PLATE 397. STAINED-GLASS WINDOW IN THE CHURCH OF SAN LORENZO BY MATHIAS GOERITZ, MEXICO, D.F.

PLATE 398. "HONEYCOMB I," CRYSTAL, PLASTIC, AND METAL FORM, 31½ X 12 IN. (80 X 30.5 CM.), BY FELICIANO BEJAR, MEXICO, D.F.

PLATE 399. HIGHWAY DIVIDER, STONE, CERAMIC MOSAIC AND CEMENT, NEAR CUERNAVACA, BY JUAN O'GORMAN

PLATE 400. "LA GUERRA," TAPESTRY BY ISAAC GUTIERIZ, TEOTITLAN DEL VALLE

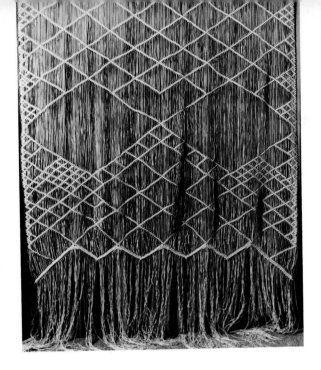

PLATE 401. WALL HANGING, MACRAME KNOTTING TECHNIQUE, 10 FT. HIGH (3 M.), BY SPENCER DEPAS, PORT-AU-PRINCE

PLATE 402. DETAIL OF CERAMIC SCREEN WALL BY JASMIN JOSEF, PORT-AU-PRINCE

PLATE 403. "MAGICIAN," STEEL SCULPTURE BY MURAT BRIERRE, PORT-AU-PRINCE

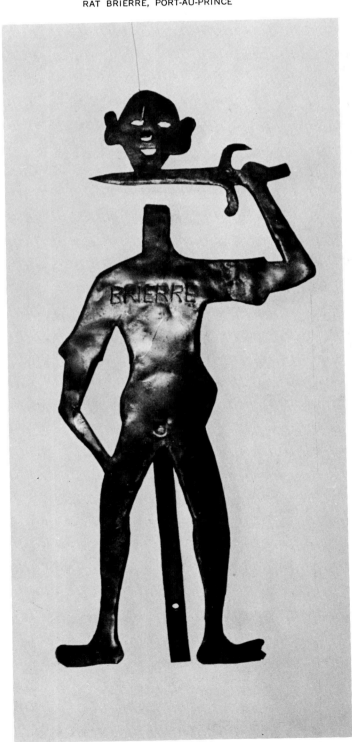

PLATE 404.   POT BECOMES A HAT FOR A POTTER'S DAUGHTER, NEVIS

PLATE 405.   FIRING CERAMIC POTS ON A BED OF TWIGS, COCONUT FRONDS, AND HUSKS, NEVIS

champlevé	champlevé
niello	nielle

Textiles	Textiles
weaving	tissage
cloth	tissu, toile, étoffe
tapestry	tappisserie
carpet, rug	tapis
decorative fabrics	étoffes decoratives
hand printed	peintes à la main
silk screened	serigraphies
block print	imprimées par gravure sur bois
lace making	dentelles
sewing	couture
embroidery	broderie
stitchery	broderie moderne
knitting	tricot
wall hanging	tapisserie murale
linen	toile, lin
wool	laine
silk	soie
cotton	coton, cotonnade
fiber	fibre

Woodworking	Travail du Bois
wood turning, carving	tourner, tailler
wood inlay, intarsia	marqueterie
furniture	mobilier
cabinetmaking	ébénisterie
lacquering	vernissure en laque

Paper	Papier
collage	collage, papiers collés
decoupage, cutouts	découpage
paper folding, (origami)	pliages
mobiles	mobiles en papier
paper sculpture	sculpture en papier